THE
GALAPAGOS
ISLANDS

REVISED & UPDATED

THE
GALAPAGOS
ISLANDS
Exploring,
Enjoying
& Understanding
Darwin's Enchanted Islands

SECOND EDITION

MARYLEE STEPHENSON

THE MOUNTAINEERS BOOKS

Published by
The Mountaineers Books
1001 SW Klickitat Way, Suite 201
Seattle, WA 98134

First edition, 1989. Second edition: first printing 2000, second printing 2004. Revised edition: first printing 2005, second printing 2006, third printing 2007, fourth printing 2008, fifth printing 2010

Distributed in the United Kingdom by Cordee, www.cordee.co.uk

Manufactured in the United States of America

Project Editor: Dottie Martin
Editor: Carol Anne Peschke
Book Designer and Layout Artist: Amy Winchester
Cover Designer: Peggy Egerdahl
Mapmaker: Jennifer LaRock Shontz
Photography: Marylee Stephenson, unless otherwise noted
Cover photograph: *Male land iguana* © Getty Images
Frontispiece: *Blue-footed booby and downy chick* © Marylee Stephenson

Library of Congress Cataloging-in-Publication Data
Stephenson, Marylee.
    The Galapagos Islands : exploring, enjoying & understanding Darwin's enchanted islands / Marylee Stephenson.— 2nd ed.
        p.   cm.
    Includes bibliographical references and index.
    ISBN 0-89886-688-X (pbk.)
        1. Natural history—Galapagos Islands—Guidebooks. 2. Galapagos Islands—Guidebooks. I. Title.
    QH198.G3 S73 2000
    508.866'5—dc21   00-009943
                                                              CIP

♻ Printed on recycled paper
ISBN (paperback): 978-0-89886-688-9
ISBN (ebook): 978-0-89886-939-2

CONTENTS

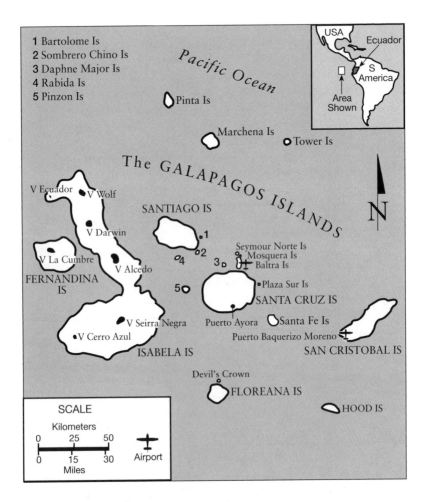

1 Bartolome Is
2 Sombrero Chino Is
3 Daphne Major Is
4 Rabida Is
5 Pinzon Is

USA
Ecuador
S America
Area Shown

Pacific Ocean

Pinta Is

Marchena Is   Tower Is

The GALAPAGOS ISLANDS

N

V Ecuador   V Wolf
SANTIAGO IS
V Darwin
V La Cumbre   1
V Alcedo   2
3   Seymour Norte Is
FERNANDINA IS   4   Mosquera Is
Baltra Is
5   Plaza Sur Is
SANTA CRUZ IS
V Seirra Negra   Puerto Ayora   Santa Fe Is
V Cerro Azul   Puerto Baquerizo Moreno
ISABELA IS   SAN CRISTOBAL IS

Devil's Crown
FLOREANA IS
HOOD IS

SCALE
Kilometers
0   25   50
0   15   30   Airport
Miles

About Island Names

Nearly all the Galapagos Islands have been known by more than one name. This book follows current Ecuadorian usage, with a few common exceptions. Alternate names of major islands are shown in parentheses in the Contents and chapter headings.

ACKNOWLEDGMENTS

The Galapagos are a very important place for me. Over the last 26 years I have made seven visits to the islands, ranging from 1 to 2 weeks each time (plus the same amount of time on the mainland of Ecuador in the rain forest and visiting various haciendas in the Highlands). I have traveled in tiny, hand-hewn converted fishing boats and luxurious motor-sailing vessels, and even a relatively small cruise ship. I have visited many sites several times and some sites only once. I interviewed staff at both the Galapagos National Park Service and the Charles Darwin Research Station on most of these visits. Each visit has had its own character. Each has been made especially enjoyable and productive by guides, crew, and staff at the Charles Darwin Research Station, the Galapagos National Park Service, and the tour companies that arranged part or all of my trips. A number of people have contributed to my enjoyment of these islands, but in particular I would like to thank Diego Andrade, the guide for my first trip. He set a standard of guiding that cannot be excelled.

As I have worked on the revisions to this edition, I have received advice, comments, suggestions, and corrections from Desiree Cruz, Ximena Cordova, and Juan Tapia, all truly excellent guides, and Roslyn Cameron, Development Manager at the Charles Darwin Research Station. I must also thank Ros and her artist son, Mason Leon, for their informal hospitality, which added greatly to my latest trip. I cannot thank enough each of these individuals and their colleagues at the Darwin Station and the park service for their efforts and patience and for all that they do for the islands in their day-to-day work (and for their art, in Mason's case).

Most of my Island trips have been arranged by Allie Almario of Myths and Mountains Travel (allie@mythsandmountains.com). She also handled a portion of the mainland Ecuador excursions. Her expertise and good humor have been invaluable in my carrying out this most enjoyable work. Also making the mainland segments most enjoyable were my friend and travel agent, Jeanneth Vasconez and her personal and business partner, Manolo Marin, as well as our guide, William Arevalo, of Servicios Turisticos Blueline, Quito, (blueline@andinanet.net).

I would like to note that the maps for the first edition of the book were prepared by Monica Jackson, and I thank her for her goodwill under tight deadlines at that time. For this revision, there have been some modifications to these maps, based on drawings provided in the Galapagos National Park's *Guide to Visitor Sites*. However, my thanks to Monica continue.

Because I operate my own consulting business, all travel schedules had to fit the constraints of my day job. Without the continuous help of Jeannie McIntosh, and then Joe Goodwill, in my office, none of this would have been possible.

Over the years, I have traveled to the Galapagos with dear friends and relatives. There have been many of them, but I would like to thank especially my first Galapagos travel companion, Pamela Sachs, and my fellow family travelers: my sister, Karey; her husband, Fredie; and my nephews, Skeeter and Cricket Griesman.

Finally, my thanks go to Kathleen Cubley, Deb Easter, Storm Yanicks, and Judy Petry for their patient efforts in bringing this revision to completion.

Naturally, although I received so much help from all these people, any errors in the book are exclusively attributable to me.

A Note About Safety

Safety is an important concern in all outdoor activities. No guidebook can alert you to every hazard or anticipate the limitations of every reader. Therefore, the descriptions of roads, trails, routes, and natural features in this book are not representations that a particular place or excursion will be safe for your party. When you follow any of the routes described in this book, you assume responsibility for your own safety. Under normal conditions, such excursions require the usual attention to traffic, road and trail conditions, weather, terrain, the capabilities of your party, and other factors. Keeping informed on current conditions and exercising common sense are the keys to a safe, enjoyable outing.

Political conditions may add to the risks of travel in Ecuador and the Galapagos Islands in ways that this book cannot predict. When you travel, you assume this risk and should keep informed of political developments that may make safe travel difficult or impossible. A number of Internet sites have travel advisories and information about political situations and health hazards (see the Planning a Visit section).

The Mountaineers Books

Adult red-footed booby

Part I
OVERVIEW

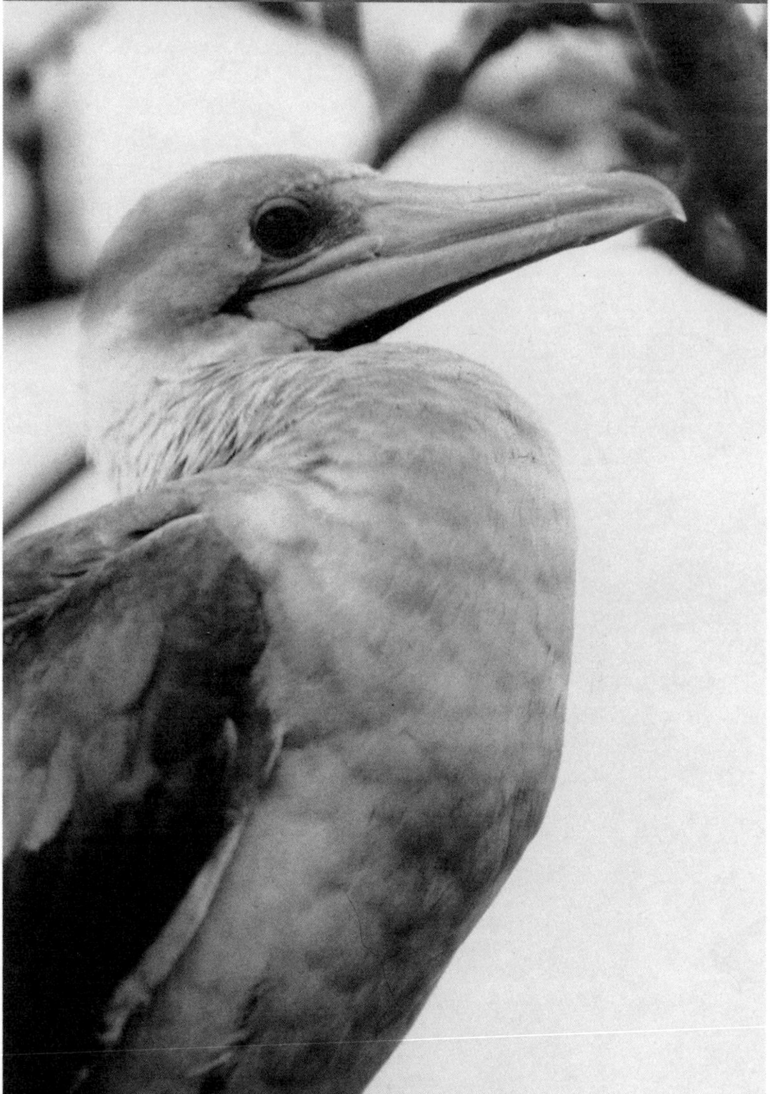

Skipper on Isabela

1
The Living Laboratory

What havoc the introduction of any new beast of prey must cause in a
country, before the instincts of the indigenous inhabitants have
become adapted to the stranger's craft or power.

Darwin, *Voyage of the Beagle*

For nearly a century and a half, since Darwin's visit in 1835, the Galapagos Islands have been recognized as a living laboratory for the study of biological evolution. Much more recently, it has become clear that these exotic islands provide two more lessons about life: how easily it can be destroyed and how difficult it is to reverse or even slow that destruction. In the face of these immense difficulties, the watchword for the Galapagos is now *restoration*. We are accustomed to thinking of conservation of a natural heritage site or preservation of its environment. But the Galapagos are so fragile, and so much the subject of negative external influences, that the day-to-day struggle of those who work on and for these precious islands is primarily to restore the original lifeforms to the state they enjoyed before centuries of human activities on the islands. Then conservation and preservation can become truly meaningful terms in this context.

The work of restoring the islands, in the face of the negative impacts of human visitation and occupation and the overlapping impacts of weather and volcanoes, is moving as rapidly as possible. There are many encouraging stories of successful research and restoration activities. Today's visitors can become a part of that success. They can do so by learning about the islands and contributing to public awareness, promoting international environmental advocacy, and supporting research and restoration in Galapagos directly.

What are the Galapagos Islands and why are they so important? The Galapagos are an archipelago, volcanic in origin, located about 1000 kilometers (621 miles) directly west of Ecuador. They straddle the equator, extending 220 kilometers (137 miles) north to south. There are five islands more than 500 square kilometers (193 square miles) in area, two islands between 100 and 200 square kilometers (38 and 76 square miles), and about 15 smaller ones, most of which can be visited. There are also dozens of tiny islets that are part of the archipelago. The smallest island that people visit is Plaza Sur, only 0.13 square kilometer (0.05 square mile).

The islands are a national park of Ecuador. More than 97% of the land mass and all of the waters within a 40-mile radius off the baseline coast of the archipelago are preserved and protected as a national park. There are several settlements in the archipelago; the largest are Puerto Ayora on Santa Cruz and Puerto Baquerizo Moreno on San Cristobal. The total population of the islands is about 28,000. The total number of visitors to the islands in 2006 was 120,000. Somewhat more than 30 percent of these visitors were Ecuadorians, a very important segment of visitors because it is Ecuadorian citizens who are most directly involved in issues of internal migration to Galapagos or extended family visitation to the islands. Their support for restoring the islands and their cooperation in preventing the introduction of foreign plants and animals is crucial to the long-range healing and conservation of the Galapagos.

Today's visitor is very much a part of Galapagos history, for tourism is both one of the greatest threats to and best hopes for preserving the quality of life of the islands—for humans, plants, and animals. To understand that statement more fully and to fit visitors in their own ecological niche in this marvelous environment, it's necessary to look briefly at the natural and human history of the Galapagos.

Far-flung islands are particularly appropriate places to study specific biological processes because their flora and fauna are less diverse than those of the older and larger continental land masses. Islands of fairly recent volcanic origin, such as the Galapagos, have had less time for soil to develop. If the lack of time is accompanied by extremely high or low rainfall in the area or by extremes of temperature (as would be the case near the earth's poles), then soil development is further retarded. Poor soil means less plant development, and hence fewer life-forms that can be supported on the land.

Just as the problems of and opportunities for survival on far-off islands are distinctive, or even unique, so may be the life-forms that evolve in such isolation. Species that are found only in a specific locale, such as the Galapagos, are said to be endemic. The Galapagos are famous for their endemic species. These products of evolution are a constant source of fascination for the visitor, whether tourist or scientist.

The fact that islands are distant from a mainland mass means that there are obstacles to transporting animal or plant life to the island's shores. Some islands, such as

Short-horned grasshoppers mating (Schistocerca sp.)

the Galapagos, are far from a continental land mass. The life-forms found on such islands are ones that can withstand the long period of exposure to the sun, wind, and salt water that the accidental journey entails. Life-forms that make a landfall, particularly early in an island's history, may find little or no soil, little or no fresh water, and few other plants or animals to provide sustenance. They may find no others of their own species, which would prevent reproduction (unless fertilization had already taken place). Plants that rely on cross-fertilization for their reproduction face the same problem.

Such obstacles to transportation, sustenance, and reproduction can skew the types and proportions of different life-forms found on islands. On the Galapagos, for instance, the largest endemic plants are tree-sized composites, relatives of the sunflower. We are used to seeing sunflowers, daisies, and their relatives nodding in the breeze in open fields, supported by stems of a few centimeters in diameter and having a height of half a meter at most, except for the cultivated varieties that can be 2 meters tall. But in the Galapagos the scalesia "trees" have woody and pithy stems that allow them to achieve great height, although they are not true trees with real bark and treelike circulatory systems. The scalesias landed in the Galapagos because the seeds of the composite family are airborne and can be blown for great distances. These plants can achieve great size because until recently they were the most successful competitor for the soil on the moist upper slopes of the larger of the Galapagos Islands, which enabled them to reach their full potential.

In the animal world of the Galapagos, the predominant forms are reptiles. Reptiles can endure long periods without food or fresh water and could be transported fairly easily from the South American mainland on the rafts of soil and vegetation carried by river and ocean currents out to sea. The giant tortoise and the land and marine iguanas have come to characterize these islands, lending biological distinctiveness and capturing public interest.

Amphibians and mammals cannot withstand weeks of baking sun and little or no food, so endemic land mammals are few, and there are no native amphibians on the islands.

There are only two types of endemic terrestrial mammals: two bat species and several rat species. There were twelve rat species, but four have become extinct because of the overwhelming competition for food and space by introduced black rats *(Rattus rattus)*. Of the Galapagos mammals, the visitor will be most aware of the marine species: the fur seals, sea lions, and several whale and porpoise species found in these waters.

Birdlife is abundant in the Galapagos. As with the plant and other animal life, the island effect can be seen. Because birds can fly great distances, many seagoing (pelagic) species are very evident, but few are found only in the Galapagos. Boobies, frigate birds, tropicbirds, pelicans, shearwaters, petrels, and noddy terns often are encountered. They are generally the same species found hundreds or even thousands of miles away in other lands and seas. The waved albatross, although it patrols thousands of square kilometers of ocean for food, is interesting in terms of endemism. It easily travels great distances, yet almost all breeding pairs in the world breed on one tiny Galapagos island, Hood/Espanola. This albatross, like most other pelagic species, is what is known as an indigenous species but not an endemic species, found exclusively there.

The endemic oceangoing bird species are much more limited in range. There are about 1,000 penguins, a species which is unique to the islands, two gull species, and a flightless cormorant. The penguins, gulls, and cormorants do not stray far from their island home. However these birds may have arrived there, they have been confined to the area ever since and have evolved into distinct species over great lengths of time.

Flightless cormorants

Proportionately more land-based bird species are endemic to the islands. Reasons for this are complex, but this situation is linked to the great distances between the islands and the mainland.

Despite the difficulties of transportation to the island and the problems of reproduction, there is a potential advantage. Those who do survive may find little competition from other organisms. A plant that had to struggle elsewhere for enough nutrients, light, and space may find a surfeit of each on a distant island not colonized by other plants or at least not by plants with very similar needs for survival.

A bird that formerly had to fly long distances over water and then dive ceaselessly just to get enough food may find rich pickings right next to the shore. A finchlike bird that fed on a few kinds of seeds may learn how to feed on insects, although in its place of origin that food was taken by woodpeckers. An animal that was preyed upon by carnivores may find itself in a location where these predators do not exist. And over hundreds of thousands of years, the newcomer may lose its genetically based wariness of the unfamiliar.

The processes of evolution, the mechanisms of natural selection, are too complex to elaborate upon here. But results that are typical of evolutionary processes can be very evident in distant islands such as the Galapagos.

Gigantism is common in these circumstances, and the islands support huge land tortoises, giant scalesia, and ferns the size of trees. Flightlessness is common; the Galapagos Islands have a flightless cormorant. Also common is a proliferation of closely related species filling distinct ecological niches only a few meters in altitude or a valley or mountaintop away. The 13 well-known species of Darwin's finches, believed to have come from a common finch-like ancestor and now each distinct in its habits and appearance, are examples of this process. Some species are found in only a few places, others in many; some overlap in their range. The four mocking-bird species endemic to the archipelago tell a similar story. And the fearlessness of the animals in the Galapagos in the face of introduced threats, such as humans, also is characteristic of animal life on distant islands.

The formation of new and different plant and animal species is called adaptive radiation. The new species adapt to fill newly available niches or to fill previously available niches in a new way.

Visitors to the islands see examples of this process at every turn. The guides are trained to point out the distinct characteristics of the plants and animals and to identify those that are endemic or indigenous. Introduced plant and animal species are evident, as is their generally negative impact.

The behavioral distinctiveness also is very clear; the animals' calm acceptance of human visitors makes a trip to the Galapagos a truly impressive and moving experience.

But these same qualities of far-flung islands can be the source of their extreme vulnerability. Shallow soil can be swept away in moments during torrential rain if the trees that anchored it have been razed for grazing by domestic animals. Fearless animals can be killed by the outstretched hand. Predatory animals that are introduced suddenly to the island can devour eggs laid in sand or burrows. There is not enough time for a species to evolve new solutions to this new threat.

Today's visitor has come just in time to the Galapagos—in time to see the effects of human interference on biological processes and to see just how quickly life can be destroyed. Yet this is also the right time to see how humans are working to arrest and even reverse that destruction, as you will learn during your visit there.

Flightless cormorant

Pirate Cave on Floreana: room for a campfire but not much more

2
Human History

The written record of the human history of the Galapagos begins with records of Fray Tomas de Berlanga, who in 1535 was Bishop of Panama and the highest representative of the Catholic church in the Spanish territories of the Americas. Fray Tomas was sent on a troubleshooting mission to Peru, under orders from Holy Roman Emperor Charles V. Tomas's ship, becalmed off the west coast of South America, drifted to what we now know as the Galapagos. Fray Tomas sent men ashore on several islands to look for desperately needed water. His description of what they saw and did has a familiar ring:

> They found nothing but seals, and turtles, and such big tortoises that each could carry a man on top of itself and many iguanas that are like serpents. [On another island] the same conditions prevailed as on the first; many seals, turtles, iguanas, tortoises, many birds like those of Spain, but so silly that they do not know how to flee, and many were caught in the hand. (Hickman, p. 19)

Much of the human history that followed is similar. People landed to search for water and rarely found it. They saw a place that was bizarre and inhospitable. They noticed the fearlessness of the animals and took full advantage of it for "sport" and for food, which meant mostly tortoise meat. It was the word for tortoise, *galapago,* that eventually stuck as the name for the islands. It replaced the earlier *Encantadas,* Spanish for "enchanted" or "bewitched." (This name apparently arose out of the baffling and treacherous currents around the islands or the peculiar light conditions and mist and fogs that made the islands appear and disappear from a distance, in a mirage-like fashion.)

Early explorers were followed by (or overlapped with) buccaneers. South America and its wealth, real and imagined, were hotly contested by the French, Spanish, and English. Naturally, the waters around it were the scene of many struggles for power and booty. The Galapagos provided a hideout for buccaneers, offering them sporadic water supplies and regular supplies of tortoise meat. This use of the islands by pirates continued through much of the eighteenth century.

The nineteenth century saw the islands exposed to the largest and most destructive wave of human visitation: the whalers. The buccaneers certainly slaughtered animals, and they introduced rats, cats, and other highly destructive animals. But for sheer numbers, no other groups were as large as the aggregate numbers of whaling ships and their crews. In one estimate, based on whaling ship records, at least 700 whaling ships plied the Pacific between 1811 and 1844. Any one ship that came to the islands took 100 to 600 tortoises on board. (Another estimate of the rate of depletion: In one 30-year period, more than 200,000 tortoises were taken from the islands.)

The tortoises were so sought after because they provided fresh meat for the long voyages. Tortoises were stacked in the holds and could live as long as a year without food or water. Considering the atrocious quality of food on most sea voyages of the time, the appeal of fresh meat is obvious.

The numbers of tortoises that originally existed on the islands must have been phenomenal to have withstood this kind of destruction for at least two centuries. But by 1846 there were no tortoises left on Floreana, and those on Rabida and Santa Fe became extinct around that time as well.

The only thing that saved the few remaining tortoises was that the same rapaciousness shown to them was applied to whales. In the mid-1800s whale stocks became so low that the whaling industry virtually collapsed. Whalers' visits to the Galapagos ended by 1865.

Of course, the explorers, buccaneers, and whalers brought with them the maritime arm of authority. Naval ships from various countries occasionally visited the islands, sometimes by accident, sometimes as part of explorations for mapping or for finding dependable locations for water or food.

It was as a part of the English Admiralty's worldwide mapping efforts that Charles Darwin came to the Galapagos for 5 weeks in 1835. As the naturalist on the *Beagle,* he visited several of the islands. He recounts in some detail the varied characteristics of the wildlife, including the notable fearlessness. His account of his visit in *The Voyage of the Beagle* is quite readable and highly recommended.

On a visit to the home of the island administrator, Darwin was told that it was possible to tell which island a tortoise came from by noting the differences in the shape of the tortoise's shell, or carapace. This circumstance and the unique forms of birdlife seem to have been seminal in Darwin's own thoughts on the role of natural selection in evolution.

If you have a chance to read the Galapagos section of Darwin's book, you should bring along photocopies of those pages. You can read Darwin's account and travel along in his footsteps here and there. Your actual path won't necessarily be the same, but you will be seeing parts of the same islands and many of the same plants and animals as he did.

By the time Darwin arrived on the islands there had already been some human settlement there. It was of a distinctly depressing sort, however. In 1832, an attempt was made to colonize the islands with reprieved mutineers from the Ecuadorian army. (Because their choice was to serve as colonists or be executed, their enthusiasm for the project can well be imagined.) Shortly thereafter, another penal colony was established on Floreana. The cruelty of the colony's overseers became notorious over the more than 100 years that it continued to exist.

Cattle on road to Floreana Highlands

The nineteenth century saw several more attempts to colonize the islands to extract salt or sulfur or to grow crops such as sugar cane. None succeeded, and when the end came to most of these projects, it was violent.

Of course, buccaneers, whalers, and colonizers didn't just take from the island; they gave. This was not out of a spirit of charity but rather the unknowing and uncaring introduction of a wide variety of foreign plants and animals. Whalers may come and go, but the goats, cats, rats, fire ants, guava plants, avocados, balsa, and coffee they brought with them—all gone wild and taking over the space and food sources of endemic species—are still in evidence today.

Toward the end of the 1800s scientific interest in the islands increased and there were periodic expeditions to the archipelago. Their goals may have been benign (although the collector mentality cannot be seen as such), but their impact on the fragile Galapagos ecosystem was not. The scientists collected specimens in large numbers, often with little or no scientific justification, while the locals readily supplied them with food from rapidly dwindling wildlife resources. Of course, the whole approach to scientific study in the field is vastly different now, with the well-being of all life-forms being of paramount importance.

The vivid accounts of some of the scientists who visited the islands in the early twentieth century led some people, particularly in Norway, to believe that the Galapagos could be another utopia. A few individuals and families tried to make a go of it, but very few succeeded. Detailed accounts of these attempts have been published.

There are a few of these European families in the islands now. A much larger number of Ecuadorian nationals came for the land that was free to whoever was willing to try farming in the difficult environment.

The islands continued to deteriorate rapidly in the next several decades as a slowly increasing population did all it could to shape the natural environment into one suitable for farming, ranching, and village living. Trees were cut to clear grazing land. Open areas were burned by accident or for agricultural reasons, then overtaken by plants that had arrived by accident on boats or had been introduced as potential crops and had spread beyond the farmers' fencing.

The new plants often succeeded too well; sometimes the land wasn't even useful for pasture because such dense thickets were formed that no domestic animals could live among them.

Where ground cover was lost, erosion of sloping land was widespread. It doesn't rain often in the Galapagos. But when it does, usually during El Niño periods, it rains in torrents that erode unprotected soil.

Wildlife was hunted, including tortoises, and the predations by introduced mammals such as cats, dogs, burros, goats, and rats continued unabated.

You will find the human history of the islands, as portrayed in the superb exhibits of the Interpretive Centre in Puerto Baquerizo Moreno, on San Cristobal, a fascinating if sometimes horrifying trip through the last 500 years. You will also learn about change and hope for the future.

3
Saying No to Destruction

Although much of the early scientific work in the Galapagos was of dubious value, at least in terms of its impact on island wildlife, scientists' activities eventually led to positive change. Progress has been slow, but is definitely occurring. However, it has been a very close call, and there are long struggles ahead.

Progress began with the 1935 Galapagos Memorial Expedition, composed of an international team of scientists visiting the islands to commemorate the hundredth anniversary of Darwin's visit. Their work was instrumental in focusing the attention of the international scientific community on the Galapagos. The Ecuadorian government passed legislation aimed at protecting island wildlife. But there were no teeth to the legislation, and further progress toward conservation was interrupted by World War II.

The decline of the 1930s, unchecked by legislation that existed but was not enforced, continued and perhaps even increased as the human population expanded slowly and the populations of introduced plants and animals grew exponentially.

But 1959 saw another landmark in the renewal of the islands: the hundredth anniversary of the publication of Darwin's *The Origin of Species*. That year, the combined efforts of Ecuadorian conservationists and international scientific and conservation groups resulted in the establishment of the two basic building blocks of the renewed Galapagos: The Ecuadorian government declared all of the islands (exclusive of already-settled areas) to be a national park, protected from all forms of destructive use, and the Charles Darwin Foundation was incorporated. The Foundation was supported by the UHCN—World Conservation Union (IUCN), among other groups and individuals. The mandate of the Foundation (and its staff at the research station on Santa Cruz) has been renewed over the years.

It was not until 1964 that the research station actually began to operate in the islands. Three years later, the Galapagos National Park Service was set up under the direct guidance of the Ecuadorian government. The first park superintendent started work in 1972, and over the years small numbers of wardens and patrol boats have been added to the service.

The collaboration of the park service and the research station makes possible inclusion of the station's expertise in scientific and conservation matters in the courses all park service guides must take before they are licensed to work on boats. The guides bring their enhanced scientific knowledge to the tourist and also make sure that animals are not disturbed and flowers not picked and that visitors clean their

Charles Darwin Research Station's raised boardwalk trail into Opuntia Forest

shoes carefully when leaving any site and boarding the boat (so that seeds from one island are not introduced to another); in general, this training helps ensure that the islands are treated with enlightened respect.

The guides also help call attention to any detrimental changes to the visitor sites on the islands. Guides are out every day in nearly every corner of the archipelago, and they notice sudden changes such as fire, volcanic eruptions, or the approach of destructive introduced animals to previously safe areas.

This kind of information is instantly reported by guides to the park service so they can respond immediately to the threat. Their experiences also contribute to long-term study of the situation so that proper decisions can be made about the best long-range responses. The Charles Darwin Foundation and the Galapagos National Park Service have worked in tandem to develop programs for predator control, captive breeding, and return of threatened species to their home islands (when it is safe to do so).

Control, much less total eradication, of wild dogs, goats, burros, cats, and rats is extraordinarily difficult, though the decades of dedicated effort are definitely paying off. Goats have been eliminated completely from most islands. Rats are a nearly intractable problem here, as they are worldwide. The battle to control or eliminate feral dogs, cats and burros is progressing successfully. In fact, donkeys have been eliminated on Santiago and from Northern Isabela. Cats have been eradicated from Baltra, the island where many visitors land.

The struggle to eradicate pigs has been successful on Santiago and as of 2001, are regarded officially as having been eradicated. This was accomplished through an intensive hunting program, with the aid of trained dogs. Eradicating pigs on this island, one of the major ones of the archipelago, has been of inestimable value for the survival and increase of native tortoises, sea turtles, Galapagos petrels, and Galapagos rails, both of the latter being cryptic, ground-nesting birds. This achievement has been made possible particularly through the support of the Global Environmental Facility (GEF), with vital "counterpart" funding from Lindblad Expeditions. This support and fundraising from passengers has been the key to this success story.

One of the most heartening stories of successful restoration has been with the tortoises of Española (Hood). In the 1960's, only 14 of these massive animals were located there. All were brought in for captive breeding. On March 26, 2000, the 1000th individual was returned to Española, an island now free of introduced species. Research has shown that by the time they are approximately 4 years old they are big enough to no longer be threatened by the introduced rats that exist on other islands.

Despite all the difficulties, the destruction of tortoises and iguanas has been brought under control, although in some cases control has been achieved only by removing the few remaining individuals and taking them to the station for breed-ing. Thus it can be said that although they have been saved, those that cannot yet be restored as a species to their natural environment remain endangered. This is true for many endemic life-forms on the islands: they may be safe at the moment, but they are still endangered because their continued existence relies so greatly on inter-ventions by scientists, park staff, and the many local, national, and international supporters of the islands.

Recent arrivals on the islands that are causing concern include a small tree-dwelling frog, *Scinax quinquefasciata,* which is known from the coastal lowlands of Ecuador. At this point, the potential impact of this amphibian stranger, one of four species recorded as arriving in cargo brought in from the mainland during the 1997–98 El Niño, is heaviest in the Isabela Island flamingo lagoons. Scientists have determined where it appears, what its potential threat is, and what are the most effective means of eradicating it—including the local community in regular frog hunts.

But with all the frustrations, the overall story of the restoration work at the research station is one of success—success in being established in the first place and in the slow, small steps that sometimes begin to reverse and sometimes even halt the ravages of the past.

GNPS interpretive sign explaining the Park's commitment to solar energy use

Two major milestones in the Galapagos story occurred 10 years apart: in 1978, when the Galapagos National Park was named a World Heritage Site by UNESCO and in 1986, with the creation of the Galapagos Marine Reserve. At this time, the protective legislation was strengthened by the proclamation of the Special Law for the Conservation and Sustainable Development of Galapagos Province. The Galapagos National Park Service administers this reserve. The Special Law is complex; and its provisions include restriction of fishing except for commercial (or artisanal, nonindustrial) use by local residents. There are ongoing efforts by the park, the Charles Darwin Foundation, and national and international stakeholders to find ways to make the ideal of the reserve become a reality for all concerned.

All of this complex and often colorful history leads us back to today's visitors and the ecological niche they occupy there. It is my belief that the sheer scientific value of the islands alone justifies preserving and managing them with the present approach. The enormous economic and prestige value of being a UNESCO-designated World Heritage Site and a significant international tourism destination also encourage the local people and the Ecuadorian government in their efforts to renew and maintain this precious resource. Access to the islands is controlled carefully, and, if it were not, there would be nothing left but a few dry rocks with a lot of rats and goats eating themselves into oblivion.

This is not to say that every islander and every environmentalist or visitor is completely satisfied with the way the park has been set up and managed. But there still is a miracle of conservation taking place, a miracle that islanders, scientists, and visitors are supporting by our presence, appreciation, learning, and contributions of time and money.

4
Geology and Topography

The whole Galapagos archipelago is spread across an area of about 130,000 square kilometers, including the land mass and surrounding waters that are also within the protected area. The Galapagos are among the most active volcanic areas in the world and are of great scientific importance. The land mass of the islands has resulted from volcanic action that built up the land in one of two ways: layering or uplift.

Most of the islands have the classic conical shape that we associate with volcanic action. Some islands have one dominant cone with small subsidiary cones littering its slopes. (Isabela, for example, has six major volcanic mountains, several of which are active.) These mountainous islands are formed through successive eruptions that build up layer upon layer of lava and ash. This can happen on existing land or underwater. If it is the latter, the mountain may eventually reach such size that its peak reaches the surface and it then appears as an island.

By contrast, a few islands, such as Plaza Sur, Baltra, and Seymour Norte, were once flat ocean bottom that was raised by shifts of molten material below. This process is called uplift, and it gives these islands their characteristic "tilted table" look.

The oldest of the Galapagos Islands are in the southeastern edge of the archipelago. Española (Hood) is more than 3 million years old. The western islands of Fernandina and Isabela, on the other hand, are less than 700,000 years old.

These islands on the western side of the Galapagos have shown the most recent volcanic activity. There was an eruption of the Fernandina volcano in 1958, obliterating the lake at the bottom of the crater (it reformed 2 years later). Then in 1968, the crater floor of Fernandina's volcano suddenly sank another 300 meters below its previous level of 800 meters below the edge of the rim. (The crater itself is 4 by 6.5 kilometers across.) On the day that the floor was subsiding, more than 200 earthquakes took place on the island. In 1977 this volcano poured out fresh lava into its cra-

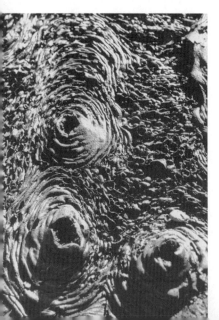

Lava bubbles in the pahoehoe flow

The Pinnacle rock on Bartolome

ter and then in 1978 it had eruptive activity again. It erupted again in 1988, 1991, 1995, and 2005.

Isabela also has a very active recent history of volcanic events. In February 1979 its southernmost volcano, Volcan Cerro Azul, erupted over a period of 3 weeks. Lava was spewed as high as 200 meters into the air. The lava flows are estimated to have reached 10 kilometers in length. It erupted again over a period of 2 months, starting in September 1998. The latest eruption was in October, 2005.

Because of their geological history, the topography of the islands is one of many moderately steep slopes, often leading to a major mountain. The height of the islands ranges from just a few meters above sea level (in the case of those that were uplifted or are simply very small) to Isabela's Volcan Wolf, which rises 1707 meters (5600 feet) above sea level. Visitors spend most of their time at the low edges of the islands, but there is usually time for a trip to the highlands of Santa Cruz or San Cristobal.

The range of altitudes has great implications for the amounts of precipitation available at greater heights and for soil development and plant and animal life.

Hornitos (Spanish for "little ovens") on the Sullivan Bay Lava Flow

Thorny rosettes on tree cactus on Sante Fe

5
Plant Life

Plant life is the basis of all life in the Galapagos, although it is often overshadowed for the visitor by the animals found there. Yet the plants often are beautiful, and they are surely as interesting. They can tell us about their evolutionary processes and the need to preserve them against destructive intruders such as other plants, grazing and rooting animals, and people.

There is no clear count of the number of plant species in the islands, but it appears that there are about 500 native "higher" plant species. Nearly half of these are endemic to the islands. There are another 500 moss, liverwort, and lichen species. Introduced plants now outnumber the native plants, with over 500 of these intruders recorded, as well as another 200 or more that are considered to be naturalized to the islands (as of 2005), often with very negative results for the native plants. The most aggressive of these introduced species, which have supplanted tens of thousands of acres of native plants on the islands, include guava, passionflower, elephant grass, blackberry, lantana, and quinine. A number of native Galapagos plants are in danger of becoming extinct on the islands and, in the case of endemic species, extinct worldwide. The park service is actively trying to control or eradicate these threats to island plant life. It is a staggering task, especially with limited budgets. Progress is certainly being made, but so much more remains to be done before success can be achieved. However, two species of blackberry were eradicated in 2005 and park staff removed many acres of quinine to facilitate the recovery of the miconia zone in Santa Cruz.

In general terms, the plant life of the Galapagos can be grouped according to ecological zones that roughly follow the altitude profiles of the islands. The location of a given spot on an island also plays a role in what type of vegetation is the most characteristic (i.e., at the shore, which might be sandy or rocky or muddy, or further inland).

COASTAL ZONE

The lowest zone is the coastal one, and it can be further divided into wet and dry subdivisions. The wet areas are the mangrove thickets that edge many of the islands. The dry subdivision is the beach and dune areas.

Mangroves have many strategies for surviving in a very harsh environment. They are awash with salty water, and they are alternately exposed to wet and dry conditions. The mud in which they anchor themselves is extremely oxygen poor.

They have special means of resisting the salt, retaining fresh water, taking oxygen directly from the air, and spreading their roots very far at the muddy surface rather than going down deep into unstable, low-nutrient earth. They are like watery forests in that they provide a sheltered home for a rich array of wildlife. Shrimp, crabs, and small fish find shelter there, and in turn provide food for larger fish and for the herons, noddies, and pelicans that lurk above waiting for a snack.

The dry area of the coastal zone includes the upper beaches themselves, especially the dune areas that are usually above high-tide levels and can support terrestrial plant life. Plant life here consists of low, spreading plants that are very good at retaining moisture and clinging to what little stable sand or soil is available. The most striking is the herb *Sesuvium portulacastrum*, which has stems that turn a brilliant rose toward the end of the dry season (roughly October to December). Seeing those mats of color on a gleaming white dune is a memorable experience. You can't miss it on Plaza Sur or on the path at Sombrero Chino.

ARID LOWLANDS ZONE

The arid lowlands zone stretches inland from an island's beaches up to about 60 meters of elevation. It is best envisioned as a desert, for except in the very moist years when the El Niño current sweeps alongside the islands, it is indeed a very dry environment. Here plants are scrubby, thorny, and sparsely spaced. They too have their strategies for retaining moisture and clinging to sandy soil.

This zone is host to some of the more striking cactus plants of the islands: the candelabra cactus

Optunia on Plaza Sur

Lava Cactus (Brachycereus nesioricus)

Jasminocereus thouarsii, the treelike prickly pear *Opuntia echios,* and the low-lying prickly pear *Opuntia helleri.* On recent lava flows such as the one at Sullivan Bay, the short tubes of the lava cactus *(Brachycereus nesioticus)* are scattered here and there.

In this dry area, it is possible to see vines such as the endemic lava morning glory *(Ipomoea habeliana)* and the endemic passionflower *(Passiflora foetida).* (An introduced species of this latter plant is causing a great deal of concern as it spreads rapidly, replacing native plants.)

As the land slopes upward, the most evident plant is the Palo Santo tree *(Bursera graveolens).* It is silvery gray, and other than having a rich collection of lichen on its surface, it looks quite dead. There are no leaves much of the time, but when the rare rainy period does come, the leaves burst out, as do its small white flowers. Many visitors' walks lead through swaths of these intriguing trees.

TRANSITION ZONE

As the zone name implies, the transition zone has plants characteristic of both the lower arid zone and the somewhat more humid levels above. In general, the vegetation is more dense and less desertlike in its appearance. There are also more species than in the arid zone.

In the category of large shrubs or smaller trees there are two common species. One is the pega pega *(Pisonia floribunda),* which is endemic to the islands. Another endemic species is the guayabillo *(Psidium galapageium),* which occurs in this zone and also farther up in the scalesia zone. It has white flowers and a small fruit like the guava, *(Psidium guajava),* to which it is related.

Less obvious but equally interesting herbaceous plants of the transition zone are the maidenhair fern *(Adiantum concinnum)* and the Galapagos tomato *(Lycopersicon cheesmanii)*, which is endemic to the islands. The latter is salt tolerant.

SCALESIA ZONE

This is the first of what are also known as humid zones, although it is named after the treelike plant that characterizes the levels between 300 and 600 meters. *Scalesia pedunculata,* the daisy tree, is endemic to the islands. It is one of the few trees in its family, the asters (order Compositae). It is an example of gigantism in island species. It ranges in height from 5 to 15 meters.

Walking in a scalesia forest is rather like walking in the rainforests of the northwest coast of North America. The trees are not as tall, but there are the great beards of moss and coats of lichen on the branches and trunks. There is a sense of stillness, of being surrounded by a rich, dense world that is a home for many kinds of life.

These scalesia forests have been seriously reduced in numbers and range by human-related activities. Pigs and goats root out the seedlings and feed on older plants. Land was cleared for planting or grazing. Fires occasionally have taken their toll. Plants such as the guava have infiltrated nearly all the highlands of the islands; their dense growth pattern squeezes out most other plants in an area.

The control of goats in some areas has allowed the scalesia to rebound, but total healing is very far away. The guava is nearly unstoppable once it has been introduced.

MICONIA ZONE

The miconia zone is the humid zone just above the scalesia zone, at about 600 to 700 meters. It is named after what once was the dominant plant of this level, *Miconia robinsoniana,* a shrub that grows 3 to 4 meters high. It is very attractive, having regular pointed leaves, with very evident grids of veins forming patterns on the shiny leaves. The leaves are shaded at their edges with yellow or red, which

Delicate mushroom on San Cristobal

adds to their appeal.

The miconia is endemic to the Galapagos and is now considered the most endangered plant in the islands. Grazing cattle have been responsible for much of its destruction on San Cristobal and Santa Cruz. You are most likely to go to a miconia area on Santa Cruz. It is a lovely experience, because much progress has been made in the protection of the land from invasive plants and in recovery of the miconia here—which is a tribute to the work of the park service wardens in particular. They regularly go to the area and hand-chop and poison the invasive quinine trees—one at a time.

Once you are in the miconia zone, look on the ground for some of the mosses that grow there. There is a very handsome club moss called Lycopodium clavatum. It grows only about 15 centimeters high, but its prickly green stems make it stand out from the surrounding vegetation beneath your feet. The miconia zone also is the home of the Galapagos cotton (Gossypium darwinii), which is endemic to the islands. It is an important nesting site for the Galapagos petrel *(Pterodroma phaeopygia)* which is a ground-nesting bird.

FERN AND SEDGE ZONE

The fern and sedge zone occurs at more than 900 meters. It is also called the pampa zone by some scholars. Overall it is the wettest zone of the islands.

Not all islands have this elevation, so some lack its characteristic vegetation. Also, the amount of rainfall determines whether the plant life in a given high-elevation location is of this type. Some slopes, protected by a mountain from the prevailing moisture-laden winds, may be too dry to have a fern and sedge zone.

These moist and high conditions are very hospitable to sedges, grasses, and ferns. Various mosses and liverworts thrive here as well. No true trees, and few shrubs, grow here. The dominant plant, in the undisturbed state, is the endemic Galapagos tree fern *(Cyathea weatherbyana)*. It is quite a shock to see that they are as tall as an adult and that they have fiddleheads as big as a fist.

Immature frigate bird

6
Birds

You don't have to be a birdwatcher to find the birdlife of the islands an endless source of enjoyment. And if you are a birdwatcher, you will find yourself in paradise.

It isn't that there is a large number of species in the islands. There are only 56 resident species, 26 regular migrants, and 71 species that are classified as accidentals. But of the 56 resident species, 44 are endemic species and sub-species. The chance to add perhaps 20 of these 44 to your life list is one of the great appeals of the trip for the dedicated birder. And this is not to forget the chance to see a large number of the other resident birds, some of which are rarely seen anywhere else in their range. The enthusiastic birder will also be interested to know that as of 2000, the Hawaiian or Dark-rumped petrel, a seabird in danger of extinction, is now considered an endemic Galapagos species and will be called the Galapagos petrel (Petrodroma phaeopygia). As of 2005, the "new" species is the Galapagos shearwater, (Puffinus subalaris.) This bird has been known in Galapagos for over 100 years, but was considered an endemic sub-species of Audubon's shearwater, and had at the time the scientific name of *Puffinus Ihermieri subalaris*.

For birder and non-birder alike, there is always the opportunity to see the birdlife up close for extended periods. From your boat deck you can watch for hours as the boobies dive for fish. A Hood mockingbird *(Mimus macdonaldi)* may land on your hat. You might have to watch your step to avoid tripping over the nest of a flightless cormorant *(Nannopterum harrisi)*. Various Darwin's finches will hop in and out of your *panga* (dinghy) or up on the bigger boat to search for tidbits. Off on the horizon a waved albatross *(Diomedea irrorata)* will be skimming the crest of the swells.

Not only is it easy to see many of the bird species found in the islands, but it is often possible to see them busily engaged in nesting. The equator does not have the clearly differentiated seasons of more temperate latitudes. The length of day is constant, and there are no strong light-related cues to set hormones racing and mate searching for mate. Temperatures on the islands are nearly constant, although in El Niño years both air and water temperatures can soar. There are wet and dry seasons, but they are ill-defined and not entirely predictable. (And "wet" and "dry" are relative terms, with "wet" often being nearer dry in terms of measurable precipitation.)

All of these factors mean that food supplies may be more evenly spaced out, and some bird species may breed more than once in a year if the nestlings have gone and there still is enough food to support a new family. In some years fish supplies are very low, and it is impossible to feed young. In other years the food supplies are very rich. The birds must respond to these circumstances as they arise, so some species are breeding at almost any time of year. In bad years, very few seabirds may come to land and breed successfully.

SEABIRDS

Nineteen seabird species breed in the islands, and three of these are endemic. The endemic ones are spectacular. There is the Galapagos penguin *(Spheniscus mendiculus)*, a type of bird we usually associate with the Antarctic and the very tip of South America or the southern shore of Australia. But here under the blast of the equatorial sun we can see this unique species carrying out its everyday life.

The flightless cormorant is endemic, as is the lava gull. The waved albatross is nearly endemic, with a very few pairs nesting on an island near the coast of Ecuador (and their status is very uncertain). The same is true for the swallow-tailed gull *(Creagrus furcatus)*, of which only a few pairs nest on an island off the coast of Colombia.

Many of the other seabirds are quite dramatic in their own ways. There are the huge and somehow ominous frigate birds (*Fregata minor* and *F. magnificens*), which are known as klepto-parasites because they live off other seabirds by stealing their food. You can often see them harassing a lava gull or booby with a fish in its beak. Suddenly, after an avian dogfight, the smaller bird drops the fish and the frigate

Lava gull

Nazca boobies

bird swoops down to snatch the morsel before it hits the water. It can do this even if it was flying several meters above the other bird. If by chance the food hits the water and sinks more than a few centimeters before the frigate bird gets to it, the frigate bird abandons the quest and another chase may soon be on.

Other birds of open water are the Nazca (formerly "masked") booby and blue-footed boobies (*Sula granti* and *S. nebouxii*). The blue-footed is seen very often because it hunts fish in the shallow sea near the shores, where the tour boats spend much of their time. The Nazca booby fishes much farther out to sea, so it is usually

Tropicbird flying with tail streaming

Pair of red-footed boobies at Punta Pitt on San Cristobal

seen at its nests on islands such as Daphne Major, Genovesa (Tower), or Española.

Many of the seabirds are ground nesters; some of these, such as the petrels, nest in burrows. The red-billed tropicbird *(Phaethon aethereus)* nests in the rocky crevices of several islands. The brown noddy nests on cliffs by the sea and in small caves. The blue-footed booby nests on the open ground on a number of the islands; they are easy to see on Seymour Norte, Daphne, and Española. Their mating behavior is a charming and amusing sight as they paddle their bright blue webbed feet up and down, throwing their wings out and head and tail up, wheezing all the while.

But the red-footed booby *(Sula sula)* actually nests in trees and shrubs. They can be seen on Genovesa, peering down on visitors from their rather shaky vantage points. The other shrub- or tree-nesting (it's hard to tell sometimes where a shrub leaves off and a tree begins in the islands) birds are both frigate bird species and the pelican *(Pelecanus occidentalis)*.

LAND BIRDS

Just as the seabirds rely on the sea for their food supply, the land birds rely on the food found on the land masses. In very general terms, the land birds follow the vegetation zones of the islands because the different plants supply the range of food used by different species. However, the division of birds into sea and land leaves out the birds that spend much of their time on the edges of the land while feeding in the shallows of the sea, the lagoons, and the few ponds and lakes of the islands. These are the flamingo *(Phoenicopterus ruber)*, four members of the heron family, the white-cheeked pintail *(Anas bahamensis)*, and two shorebirds, the American oystercatcher *(Haematopus palliatus)* and the common stilt *(Himantopus himantopus)*.

Aside from the birds living at the edges of water, 28 land bird species breed on the Galapagos. Twenty-six of them are endemic, a very large proportion of the whole avian repertoire of the islands. This includes the Galapagos petrel and Galapagos shearwaters. In types they range from the endemic Galapagos hawk *(Buteo galapagoensis)* to two members of the rail family that live in the moist, dense highlands of several islands, an endemic dove *(Zenaida galapagoensis)*, a cuckoo, two owl species, two flycatchers, one warbler, four mockingbirds, and the 13 species of the Darwin's finches.

A trip of at least 1 week should allow you to see the great majority of the land birds. It will be difficult to locate and identify each of the Darwin's finches, but with a good guide on board and careful attention to the bird guidebook, you should be able to see at least half of them. In any case, it will be very clear that they are different in looks and behavior.

Sea lion basking on Rabida Island Beach

7
Mammals

The mammals of the Galapagos can be grouped according to whether they depend on the sea or the land for food. One further distinction is that between the native and the introduced species. The latter are more numerous in types and in absolute numbers, and they play a very different role in the islands than do the native mammals.

MARINE MAMMALS

Two marine mammals breed and live much of their lives in the islands. They are both in the eared seal family; one is the sea lion *(Zalophus californianus wollebaeki)*, a subspecies of the California sea lion, and the other is the endemic fur seal *(Arctocephalus galapagoensis)*.

The sea lion, often seen by visitors, is by far the larger of the two, with the mature males weighing as much as 250 kilograms. The females are appreciably smaller but still very sturdy. Estimates of the number of sea lions in the islands range from 15,000 to 50,000.

The sea lions congregate in groups of females and their pups, with a bull sea lion patrolling the territory that his family group occupies. These territorial groupings are highly fluid and stay under the sway of a particular male for only 2 weeks or so.

Younger males who do not have their own territories and family groups gather in what are called bachelor groups. As they grow older and more assertive they are able to establish their own relationships with females and set up their own territories. They may do this by raiding an existent group when the leading male is off feeding or squabbling with another male.

Sea lions are very active during the day, especially in the morning and in the late afternoon. They congregate in large numbers on sandy beaches, open rocky shores, or areas a few dozen meters inland but with easy access to the water.

Pups are born most months of the year except April and May. This means that a visitor has a very good chance of seeing pups suckling noisily or playing in the waves. When you are swimming, it is not uncommon to have these curious creatures swooshing right next to you.

The Galapagos fur seal is the smallest of the fur seals found in the southern hemisphere, and it is the only one that lives in tropical waters. Unlike other fur seals, it does not spend most of its time in the water, migrating from one area to another for

Bull sea lion amid glowing sesvuim

food or for breeding. These seals spend their lives around the archipelago, with about 30 percent of their time being spent on land. They have a number of strategies for withstanding the extreme heat and dryness of the coastal zone. For example, they spend much of their day in the cool of rocky shores and cliffs, where they can get out of the sun. They also feed mostly at night, catching squid and some fish.

There are estimated to be about 15,000 fur seals in the islands. They breed on most of the islands and can be found on or around most of them. They have their pups between June and December, which tends to be the cooler time of year and the time of the greatest food supply.

Visitors do not see the fur seal nearly as regularly as they do the sea lion, but at one or two sites, such as the fur seal grottos on Santiago, there are excellent opportunities to view them up close.

Other marine mammals can be seen in the Galapagos, but they are not land-based for breeding and other activities, as are the sea lion and fur seal. These other marine mammals are the whales, dolphins, and porpoises that frequent the waters of the archipelago. Most commonly the visitor will see the bottle-nosed dolphin *(Tursiops truncatus)* racing alongside the boat or even riding the bow waves. It is

Sea lions relaxing in pools on Mosquera Island

easy to photograph them because they may accompany a boat for many minutes at a time. (Use a polarizing filter if you have one.)

Whales, such as the humpback and orca (killer whale), are less often seen, but a lucky visitor may spot them.

LAND MAMMALS

Land mammals are not likely to be able to make the long and dangerous trip to far-flung islands; thus it is not surprising that the (surviving) native mammals include two flying ones (bats) and four rat species.

Rats are among the most resilient of all animals and evidently could survive the trip on the mats of vegetable matter that are assumed to have drifted from mainland Ecuador to the islands. A dense mat of a few square meters would provide them with enough shade, moisture, and food to make the trip.

It is thought that there were 12 rat species native to the islands. However, the introduced black rat has all but obliterated the native rats. The rediscovery in 1998 of the endemic Santiago rice rat was an exciting surprise, however, because it was believed to be extinct. Visitors are not likely to see the endemic rats, but it is quite common to see the introduced black rat around human habitation.

The two endemic bats are little known and seldom seen.

The introduced mammals have been discussed before in terms of their negative impact on the environment of the islands. Their different and highly predatory modes of feeding and breeding and their own caution in the face of humans—as when hunters are used to reduce the goat population—make non-native mammals a uniformly destructive segment of the mammal population. In some of the sites you visit, your guide can readily point out the impacts of feral rats, dogs, cats, pigs, cattle, horses, and goats. The town areas are often the places where the negative impacts are most apparent. These views are dispiriting but essential for your awareness of the complexities of the ecosystem and the daunting nature of restoring threatened and endangered island life-forms.

Young fur seal

Nonpoisonous Galapagos snake

8
Reptiles

The totem animal of the Galapagos Islands is the giant tortoise (*Geochelone ssp.*, with 11 species of the original 15 still existent). There are also sea turtles that occurs widely in the surrounding waters.

The giant tortoises can weigh 250 kilograms and measure 150 centimeters across the shell. They look slow and awkward, but they can move quite rapidly and are amazingly flexible in their movements. The most obvious way to distinguish a particular race from the others is by the size and the shape of the shell, or carapace. The *relatively* smaller ones (with saddlebacks) are found on Española and Pinta, and the largest (dome-shaped) ones are found on Santa Cruz and Isabela's Alcedo Volcano. The others range between these two ends of the physical spectrum.

The cousin of the tortoise, the Pacific green turtle *(Chelonia mydas agassisi),* uses the lagoons of the islands for breeding; the females lay their eggs in the sand of several island beaches. This mode of reproduction leaves the turtles very vulnerable to predation. Introduced rats destroy nests and eat eggs, and hatchlings making their way to the sea are taken by native predators such as hawks, herons, mockingbirds, and frigate birds. Once they reach the sea, sharks and fish prey on them. Those that do make it to open water safely and survive for the next several years will return to the lagoons and beaches of their origin and reproduce as best they can there. The visitor is most likely to see these turtles during their mating activities at sites such as Caleta Tortuga Negra, on Santiago.

The tortoises have suffered terribly from the direct predations of people, from explorers to farmers, who took tortoises in almost unbelievable numbers. Even today, poaching remains a problem.

Tortoises have also suffered from the indirect impact of people. Introduced grazing mammals such as goats and burros out-competed them for food. And because tortoises lay their eggs in the ground, the eggs and hatchlings are eaten by rats or trampled by burros. With all those attacks on their existence, the results are hardly surprising. There were once hundreds of thousands of tortoises on the islands; there are now somewhat more than 25,000. The greatest known surviving concentrations are on Alcedo Volcano and Darwin Volcano, both on Isabela and in the highlands of Santa Cruz. It is on walks to these highlands that you are most likely to see them in their natural state. Of course, at the Charles Darwin Research Station you have a wonderful view of the tortoises that are being raised as part of the restoration effort. It's great to see the tortoises up close like that, from tiny ones less than

Giant tortoise at Charles Darwin Research Station

a year old to huge aged adults.

The establishment of the national park and the combined work of the park service and the Charles Darwin Foundation can be credited with saving the species and individuals that remain. Today 10 of the 11 species are no longer considered endangered, in the sense that they are being bred and raised to maturity. However, they *are* still endangered in terms of the difficulties they face in being able to survive and increase in substantial numbers in their *natural* environment. They must still be very carefully reared, returned where possible, and carefully guarded on their home territory. The species *Geochelone abingdoni* has only one known living individual, the renowned Lonesome George. He is being cared for at the research station, in the hope of finding a female somewhere in the world, or when George goes, this species will be extinct.

Almost as well known as the giant tortoise are the iguanas, marine and land, and much less well known are the seven lizard species, three snake species, and seven gecko species.

The iguanas of the islands are very striking in both looks and behavior. They are members of the lizard family. The best known is the endemic marine iguana *(Amblyrhynchus cristatus)*. It is the only truly marine lizard in the world. They can reach a length of 100 centimeters and weigh as much as 8 kilograms.

They spend much of their time resting in large groups on rocky shores, soaking up

Sante Fe's special land iguana (C. pallidus)

the sun, expelling salty residue through their nostrils. But when they need to eat, the females and young leave their rocks and swim to nearby patches of seaweed and graze on them. The males swim further out to sea to feed.

They are ground-nesting animals, the female laying eggs in the burrow she has dug. Unlike the sea turtles, the females stay around their nests for a week or so to guard them from predators. Of course, even with the guarding activity, the nests and hatchlings are subject to the same sorts of predation as those of the sea turtles.

Although there is just one marine iguana species, there are seven subspecies. You can see how they differ in size and appearance in some locations. For example, you can see clearly that the iguanas near the fur seal grottos on Santiago are much smaller and more uniformly black than the larger ones of Española, which have great splashes of deep red on their sides.

There are two land iguana species on the islands (*Conolophus subcristatus* and *C. pallidus*), both of which are endemic. They are quite different in looks and habits from their marine counterparts. They tend to be solitary, whereas the marine iguanas are highly gregarious and gather in large groups in their resting places. They are much bulkier than the marine iguanas, which are quite sleek by comparison. They are generally yellow, with brown or black shading on the back ridge. The species *C. pallidus* is found only on Santa Fe; *C. subcristatus* is found on Fernandina (which has the largest population of them), Isabela, Santiago, Santa Cruz, Baltra, and Plaza Sur. It is on Plaza Sur that the visitor is most likely to see the latter species, dotting the landscape like huge yellow flowers. They feed on the portulaca there and gnaw through the spiny paddles of the opuntia cactus without any hesitation.

On visits to Santa Fe, your guide usually can find some individuals of the *C. pallidus* species. They are few in number but great to see. Mostly they are just splayed out in the dust, blinking occasionally at the visitors peering down at them.

Hood's distinctive lava lizard with large, colorful, stumpy tail

The lava lizards of the islands are often seen by visitors, although it is not easy to distinguish one species from another. They are small (about 25 centimeters), attractive animals but not very colorful except for the brilliant splash of orange on the throat of the female. They feed on insects and some plants.

The geckos are not well known and are seldom seen. One obvious reason is that they are nocturnal, so boat-based visitors would have little opportunity to see them. There are six species, five of them endemic.

The snakes of the Galapagos, all nonpoisonous, are seen occasionally by visitors. About a meter long when fully grown, they feed on lava lizards, marine iguana hatchlings, some bird nestlings, and rats. In turn, the snakes are preyed on by feral cats and the Galapagos hawk.

Sally Lightfoot crab at Punta Cormoran on Floreana

9

Underwater Life

The underwater life of the Galapagos is receiving increased attention from scientists, conservationists, and visitors who come on diving trips. It is the largest single habitat in the islands. It is astonishingly rich and varied, and it shapes the quality of all other life in the islands.

The Galapagos are at the convergence of three major oceanic currents—the north equatorial, the equatorial (Cromwell), and the Humboldt (Peru) coastal currents—placing them at the juncture of great underwater rivers that have differing temperatures, lateral and vertical directions, and kinds and amounts of plant, animal, and chemical content. All of this adds up to an extremely rich environment that is home to an unimaginable array of underwater life.

The generally cool waters and concomitant dryness of the land occasionally are interrupted by the near approach of a current of warm water that usually does not swing down from its ordinary path on the west coast of Central America. When this current, known as El Niño, dips near the islands, it causes temporary but drastic changes in the ocean life, in the lives of animals that depend on the ocean for food, and in the weather and everyday life of all the plants and animals of the islands.

Warm water is nutrient poor. It holds less oxygen than an equivalent volume of cold water, and with less oxygen there is less underwater plant life (phytoplankton). Less plant life means less food for underwater animal life, from the tiniest crustacean to the biggest shark or whale. Less underwater animal life means less food for seagoing mammals and birds. All of these factors converge during El Niño events.

In El Niño years water temperature soars from its usual 16°C to 20°C to nearly 30°C. The effect on all sea life is dramatic. The changes in surface temperatures and weather also are enormous. The islands are inundated with downpours. Land is washed away. Plants blossom that haven't done so for years. Seabirds may have so little food that they do not even attempt to nest. Sea lion and fur seal colonies may succeed in raising only very few young, if any. By contrast, land birds such as the finches may find themselves with so much food that they raise four or five broods over just a few months.

Until recently, it seemed that a strong El Niño event came only every 13 years or so, but over the last decades it has been occurring more frequently. A great deal of research is being done to determine the effects of the El Niño itself and the added effects of its increased frequency. El Niño is nothing new to the islands, and as devastating as it may seem, most life bounces back very quickly. However, there are concerns that the recent trends in the frequency of these currents will make it more difficult for plants and animals to recover if they are hit again with such an event within 2 or 3 years. In this case, the endemic species can be at an even greater disadvantage in the competition with introduced plants and animals.

The marine life of the islands has been little studied (although this is changing with the establishment of the marine reserve status), but it does seem clear that the surrounding waters also exhibit the same high proportion of endemic species. Plant life in the surrounding waters has been estimated to include about 360 species, with 16 percent of these being endemic.

There are an estimated 800 mollusk species, with 17% percent being endemic. There are also 24 sea urchin species, 28 sea stars, and 30 sea cucumbers.

For the typical visitor, all this underwater life is little seen, although more and more divers are enjoying this beautiful undersea world. The life of the inter-tidal zone (the areas at the water's edge that appear and disappear with the tides) is very evident to any visitor, however. The most obvious residents of these wave-splashed areas are the crabs. The Sally Lightfoot *(Grapsus grapsus)* is one of 100 crab species in the islands, but its brilliant reds and purples make it the most easily seen. The younger ones are nearly black, but the older ones, which reach the size of a human hand, become a bright orange that really stands out in contrast to the black lava rocks they so often haunt.

In contrast to the striking coloration and size of the Sally Lightfoot crab is the ghost crab *(Ocypode albicans)*. Its name comes from its pale, almost translucent coloring, which can make it hard to pick out as it scuttles along the sand. We saw thousands of them once, on the beautiful beach at the east side of Floreana's Punta Cormoran. They are only a few centimeters in size but well worth a look if you can get close enough to one.

To see more sea life, try snorkeling. Snorkeling is easy to do if the water is calm, and even a few minutes can give a very strong sense of the variety and beauty of the marine life. It is also possible to scuba dive in the islands, but be sure to book this completely through your travel agent before you leave home (see Part III, Travel Tips).

It is interesting to see how the recent inclusion of the waters of the archipelago within the park framework affects both the underwater life itself and the experience of the visitor, not to mention the residents of the islands and international commercial fishing companies. The commercial use of the marine resources, such as sea cucumbers, has been a very contentious issue, calling for every bit of negotiating and management skill available in the islands, the Ecuadorian government, and the international environmental community. In fact, as of 2005, the sea cucumber is considered to be on the point of commercial collapse. Meanwhile, you as a visitor are likely to find that your guide will devote more time than would have been the case before this boundary change in acquainting you with the marvels of the underwater life of the islands.

Frigate bird cooling off in the heat of an El Niño year

Part II
MAJOR ISLANDS
AND VISITOR SITES

1
Introduction

On a typical 3- to 8-day visit to the islands, a group usually is taken to two visitor sites each day. The captain of the boat must operate within the framework of a trip plan, which is filed with the administrative authorities of the park and the Ecuadorian navy. Some sites can be visited by all boats, including those that carry the maximum allowable load. Some sites, such as Daphne Major and Genovesa, can be visited less frequently and only by boats that carry small groups. Some sites are always visited because of their accessibility to one of the two airports. Other islands are rarely visited because of their great distance from the central islands.

Within the framework of the captain's authorized trip plan, the speed of the boat, the number of crew, and especially the sophistication of the navigational equipment, all play a large part in how many sites can be reached. Other factors include the weather, winds, and currents. Some days more than two places will be visited. On rare occasions, you will spend most of the day in transit before a far-flung destination is reached.

But given the potential fascination (or discomfort) associated with boat living, it is important to think of that travel time as an active, integral part of experiencing the islands.

BALTRA

Baltra is not an official visitor site where the visitor is told by the naturalist guide what is special about its flora and fauna. But it is one of the two airports in the islands, so it may be your first landing site. At the airport itself, there is a reception center, a waiting area, and a canteen. At the reception kiosks, visitors pay their park entry fees ($100 U.S. as of early 2000), having filled out their entry forms on the plane before arriving. It is usually a scene of happy scrambling and confusion, but you can't get lost. It is essential to keep any papers given out there, including a colorful sheet of paper with your name and a Galapagos stamp on it. You may be asked to show it before you leave the islands.

As you finish the formalities and wander blinking into the bright sun, a member of your boat crew will be waiting outside, calling out the name of your boat (which you will already know from your tour operator or travel agent). Buses provide the brief ride to the harbor, where the boats await their passengers.

But even this rather hectic beginning leaves some space for absorbing the flavor of the islands. First, if your flight is approaching the islands during the *garua* (wet and misty) season (approximately June through December), it is likely that there will be masses of low-level clouds. These are the high-overcast skies that protect you to some degree from the sun but can make photography difficult. There isn't much rain (except in the times of the El Niño), but these clouds foretell heavy mists and a chill to the air at times, particularly in the evenings. As the islands show through, they look mostly coppery-brown and gray and rugged. Regular, conical shapes predominate, from hillocks to mountains.

The large number and various sizes of islands usually come as a surprise to visitors. The shorelines gleam white, and the near-shore water is the turquoise blue so often associated with tropical islands. The final approach takes you over Mosquera, a brilliant white sandspit that you may be able to visit later.

Cooks must be ultra-efficient in small spaces.

As you stand around waiting, look a little farther to the scrub areas nearby. You are sure to see the first Darwin's finches of the trip scrabbling around on the ground. A couple of different beak sizes will be evident, and so will be the browns of the females and the blacks of the males. There won't be time here for much more than a glance, but when you reach the boats you will meet two continuously interesting and important parts of the trip: the food and the blue-footed boobies.

The cook on any boat rapidly assumes great importance, in my experience, and maintains it for the rest of the trip. Passengers are assigned their quarters, start putting away their gear, and then come up for food and sun. There's usually an excellent lunch of soup, bread, fish, a salad of fresh vegetables or fruit, and cold drinks. The cost of the food is included in the whole trip fare, but after the first free drink a running tab is kept of each person's beverage consumption. (You pay up on the last day.) This is the time to take your seasick pills (although it is best to have started the morning before leaving the mainland and then take another one on the boat) and then to go out on the deck and watch the boobies. There also should be a safety briefing at this time, and the guide will tell you about the park rules for behaving appropriately, in a careful manner, throughout the park.

In this harbor, as in nearly all sheltered water, boobies are busy fishing or standing basking on rocks. The first sight of a booby's wheeling plunge into the aquamarine sea seems to signal that your island adventure has really begun. Pelicans may join the boobies in their hunt, and lava gulls often come to sit on the *panga*, the motorboat that is tied to the larger boat. Even a sea lion may hop up into the *panga*, just a few meters away. Everyone calls everyone else over to come and look, but the sea lion generally is oblivious to the attention.

Tortoise on Sante Fe

2
Santa Cruz and Nearby Sites

S anta Cruz is located near the center of the Galapagos archipelago. Because Baltra Island is very near and many visitors land at the airport there, Santa Cruz and the islands nearby often are the first sites visitors see. Puerto Ayora is the main settlement on Santa Cruz. You'll enjoy a visit to Puerto Ayora, and your

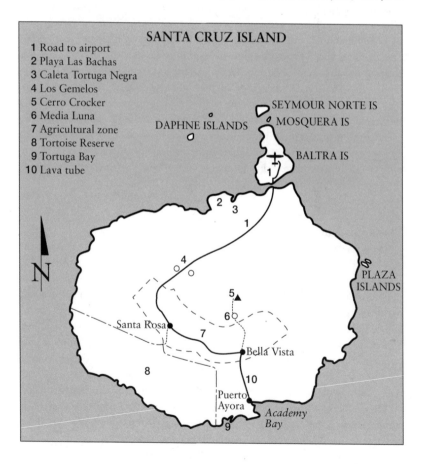

SANTA CRUZ ISLAND

1 Road to airport
2 Playa Las Bachas
3 Caleta Tortuga Negra
4 Los Gemelos
5 Cerro Crocker
6 Media Luna
7 Agricultural zone
8 Tortoise Reserve
9 Tortuga Bay
10 Lava tube

DAPHNE ISLANDS

SEYMOUR NORTE IS
MOSQUERA IS
BALTRA IS

PLAZA ISLANDS

Santa Rosa

Bella Vista

Puerto Ayora

Academy Bay

N

itinerary probably will include side trips into the moist highlands of the island.

A number of small islands are reached easily from Santa Cruz, including tiny Plaza Sur and Mosquera, with its glaring white beach and warm protected waters (great for swimming). Not far from Santa Cruz to the south is Santa Fe. It has one of the most appealing coves for anchorage and a good swim in calm water. Santa Fe also offers a great chance to see the giant cactus trees up close, and with luck you'll see some of the land iguanas that are found only there.

SANTA CRUZ (INDEFATIGABLE)

Santa Cruz is the hub of the islands for the visitor. It is centrally located, has many visitor sites, and is the home of the Charles Darwin Research Station and the headquarters of the Galapagos National Park Service. It also is the most developed village in the islands in terms of amenities for the visitor. Your group may stay overnight in a small hotel there, you can eat in one of several modest restaurants, and there are several stores where you can do some tourist-style shopping (tee shirts, postcards, etc.; some of the Otavaleño Indians from the highlands of mainland Ecuador have stalls where they sell their woolen goods such as sweaters, rugs, and tapestries). Some visitors to the islands do not come in groups, especially inveterate youthful world travelers hiking their way around or Ecuadorians who are taking a few days to visit friends or families or just taking a little vacation to the islands. For these visitors, there are local tourism operations that provide day trips to nearby visitor sites, diving services, or walking day trips to the highlands of Santa Cruz.

Playa Las Bachas

Playa Las Bachas often is the first stop for all boats that have taken on passengers from the Baltra airport. The ride is only an hour or so from the first harbor, so Las Bachas is reached in mid- to late afternoon. It is a wet landing, where the *panga* pulls into shallow water or right up on shore and then everyone hops out. It's best to carry your lightweight walking shoes and disembark barefoot. The beach is sandy, and because the cove is sheltered, the water is rarely rough, so it's an easy landing.

Las Bachas is a sudden immersion into one of the most typical Galapagos shoreline environments. First, there is the beach, in this case with white sand (others may have red or black). This beach is a major egg-laying site for sea turtles. The name *Las Bachas* refers to the indentations left in the sand by laying turtles or departing hatchlings.

Where the beach rises to a low crest, there is a band of tangled saltbush (*Cryptocarpus pyriformis*) and even the prickly pear cactus (*Opuntia helleri*). Next you approach a slight depression that holds brackish water.

On the shore and in the bushes, you will almost certainly see your first marine iguanas. They sit quietly, occasionally doing push-ups in place if they become agitated. It's easy to take pictures, although you should take care to compensate for the blackness of the iguana's skin in comparison with the glaring white sand.

I once took some good pictures, very close, of a lone marine iguana. What I managed to disguise by the close-up was the fact that it was nearly a crowd scene. Six other people ringed the iguana and four different languages were being spoken—quietly but excitedly—as we all clicked away.

Past the beach, at the lagoon, there is a good chance that there will be a couple of shorebird species (common stilt, *Himantopus himantopus,* or wandering tattler, *Heteroscelus incanum*) and—most impressive—flamingos *(Phoenicopterus ruber).* The bird guide to the Galapagos points out that the flamingos are some of the shyest island birds and that every effort should be made not to disturb them. Usually at Las Bachas it is possible to hang back at the edge of the bushes and acquire a little camouflage. Your guide will be speaking in a low voice to minimize disturbance and to set an example for others.

On your return to the beach area, some of the group may want to do a little snorkeling; it is a nice, quiet place to try this. Ask your guide beforehand whether there will be time.

Your return to the *panga* will mark the first time for an important Galapagos ritual: foot cleaning. It is imperative that you wash off any sand, seeds, or other debris from your feet and shoes. This is to prevent the artificial transport of plant life from one island to another and to help keep the boat clean. Sand can pile up very quickly and become an irritant on a well-populated boat.

Flamingo at Playa Las Bachas

Puerto Ayora

The town of Puerto Ayora is the one settlement usually visited by all tourists. Puerto Ayora is of particular interest to the conservation-oriented visitor because the headquarters of both the Charles Darwin Research Station and the Galapagos National Park Service are located there. It is also a supply center for the boats, which come in here between trips or halfway through very lengthy trips to replenish supplies. Some trip plans include just a short day (or even less) in town, visiting the Charles Darwin Research Station and perhaps taking a ride into the interior to visit a farm or to walk through the lava tubes or in the Tortoise Reserve. In either case, the stay is too short to get more than a superficial idea of how the 15,000 or so local residents carry out their daily lives.

Over the 24-year span of my visits to the islands, Puerto Ayora has evolved dramatically. It was once a rather unkempt, almost sleepy village and now it is an attractive, thriving town. The space around the main dock has been upgraded to a very attractive park-like area that you will want to spend some casual time in. The main street is paved in cobblestone, and not far along it, there is a small waterfront park with a gigantic cement waved albatross sculpture (perfect for "I was there" snapshots), and buildings have been upgraded but without losing their local color. Of course, much of the activity is oriented to tourists, but Puerto Ayora has not lost its sense of local life. For example, on your walk to the Charles Darwin Research Station, passing another huge statue, this time of a tortoise, there will be uniformed schoolchildren chattering as they go in groups to school or home, or sailors and locals playing their high-powered form of volleyball in the courts by the water. Try to find a little time just to walk or sit on one of the benches under a shade tree and enjoy

Municipal dock at Puerto Ayora

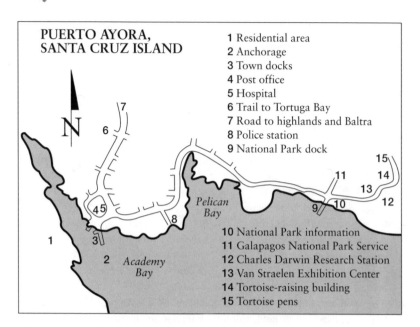

PUERTO AYORA, SANTA CRUZ ISLAND

1 Residential area
2 Anchorage
3 Town docks
4 Post office
5 Hospital
6 Trail to Tortuga Bay
7 Road to highlands and Baltra
8 Police station
9 National Park dock

10 National Park information
11 Galapagos National Park Service
12 Charles Darwin Research Station
13 Van Straelen Exhibition Center
14 Tortoise-raising building
15 Tortoise pens

a few moments of quiet and unobtrusive observation.

When you are on the go, there are many small stores in town, a few snack bars, a bank, a medical facility, a school, churches, and a small navy emplacement. You can mail your postcards in town; all mine mailed from here made it to their destinations. Nearly all stores and restaurants have postcards, and many of the small businesses carry attractive Galapagos tee shirts. There are also a number of internet cafes and phone booths.

If you've discovered you want something special to eat on the boat (it was more hot chocolate on one of my trips) or you need another tape cassette, you will find it easily in Puerto Ayora. The people are very friendly and helpful and do not seem to be tired of tourists.

Charles Darwin Research Station

The Station is an easy 1.8-mile walk from the municipal dock if you landed there. It can take up to an hour to walk to it. You could get there sooner, but you'll probably make stops along the way. The route to the station is along one of the two principal roads through the town, a comfortable walk on cobblestone pavement, with interesting town life to see. After your visit to the station you might have time for a cool drink at one of the hotels, little restaurants, or snack bars along the way. People do a lot of souvenir shopping on their way back.

If your group happens to have been let off at the national park dock, which is usually the plan, you'll visit the research station first and then saunter down through town. You'll be met there and return to your boat from the municipal dock.

Either way, the road also takes you near the edges of the mangroves that line the shore of the outskirts of Puerto Ayora. Keep a close lookout for lava herons fishing here and there. Lava lizards abound alongside the road, and marine iguanas often are seen in the low-lying mangrove areas near the entrance to the station.

Just before the station itself is the local cemetery on your left. All of the graves are above ground, and there are edifices of many shapes and sizes for containing the departed. On my last visit the cemetery had just been through its yearly renewal, for the "Day of the Dead," when the families and friends of the dead come to clean and refresh the whole area out of respectful memory of their loved ones. The buildings gleamed white, there were new flowers everywhere—artificial and real— and it was a festive but sobering glimpse of the life of the Galapagos people.

As you enter the grounds of the station, there is a very attractive gift shop along the road, on your right. It is run by the National Park Service and sells postcards, posters, books, clothing, and other Galapagos memorabilia. Proceeds from the shop go toward supporting the work of the park service.

Then you move along to the main buildings. Whenever possible, the Charles Darwin Foundation staff holds informal briefings about the islands, for visiting groups, in the attractive Van Straelen Visitors Center. (There are rest rooms in this building, by the way.) You can ask questions and be brought up to date on the latest restoration efforts that the station and park staff are working on. However, budgetary constraints have tended to limit these "briefings" but you may be fortunate enough to have one even so. There is also a very attractive video on the islands' history and the efforts to restore and renew them. There are some exhibits in the hall about the natural history of the islands.

Next you probably will go to the tortoise rearing and observation areas. (The restrooms are here, also.) You will see a number of enclosures where the young ones are being nurtured until they are old enough to be released safely on their home islands. Recall that 14 surviving adult tortoises were taken from Española in the late 1960s because their situation was

Galapagos hawk on Galapagos National Park shop roof

so precarious. The reintroduction of more than 1500 young but sturdy juveniles to the island is truly inspiring. The gift shop is also in this area, and 100% of the profits support scholarships and the station's conservation work. It is a great place to pause and purchase—for a great cause.

For the other tortoise populations, eggs are collected from their traditional laying sites, brought in, incubated, and hatched. You will see several different species on display. (Larger numbers are raised in pens beyond the areas that are not accessible to the public.) The very young tortoises you will see are from 1 to 5 years old; a typical 5-year-old measures about 30 centimeters across. Their carapaces have numbers on them to help keep track of their progress. After 5 years, a tortoise usually is big enough to survive on its home ground if its natural food supply is sufficient and it is now large enough to escape being eaten by rats. Like many of the iguanas being raised for conservation purposes, some tortoises cannot be returned to their original homes until ways are found to reduce or eradicate the threats to their survival.

The next area that can be visited is an open compound that contains huge adult tortoises in several different enclosures. Visitors can enter the largest enclosure and walk right up to the tortoises as they feed and sleep and drink from the artificial pond. It is a great place for photographing, but you are asked to refrain from touching the tortoises, tempting though this may be. This is the home of Lonesome George, too. There are signs pointing out his own compound area, and you can think for a few moments about his being anywhere from 90 to 150 years old, the very last of his race in the entire world.

This visitation area generally is a very busy place, but with all the people there, it is still possible to observe very closely how the tortoises move and feed and even doze with head resting on outstretched foot. (How do they avoid the cactus spines when they chew? Tough gums, we're told.) My favorite sight there is the yellow warblers darting around the tortoises, drinking their water, snacking on the occasional insect drawn by the tortoises' food. These tiny golden jewels contrast so sharply with the massive, slow-moving tortoises that it is somehow very moving to see them together.

The station grounds have been transformed dramatically over the years to bring the visitor closer to the lowlands habitat in which the station is situated. Wonderful elevated boardwalks snake back into the thick brush, studded with huge opuntias like those you will see on Santa Fe or Plaza Sur. These boardwalks make for one of the most beautiful, comfortable, and non-intrusive experiences of the lowland habitat. There are shaded patios at several locations along the pathways. Take a few minutes to sit and just enjoy a moment of quiet contemplation of these exotic surroundings. The boardwalks also are excellent places for picking out finches, lizards, warblers, and the occasional hawk.

The Galapagos National Park Service has its headquarters in the same area, just beyond the main parts of the research station. It is not an official visitor site, but if you get a chance to take a peek at their grounds, along with the office buildings, you will see an extremely attractive patio area that has lovely sculptured combination artworks and benches. The paintings of local land and marine life are quite beautiful and a definite addition to the working environment of the park service.

The Highlands

Many of the islands' visitor sites are very near sea level, so there are not many opportunities to experience the moist, lush island habitat at elevations between 900 and 1500 meters. Santa Cruz is the most likely place to go because of its central location and its fully developed vegetation zones, which are accessible by motor vehicle.

Most tours include a trip to the Highlands as a regular part of their itinerary. The jumping-off points for the trails into interesting highland areas—the pit craters called Los Gemelos, the lava tubes on private property that can be visited for a very small fee, the crater called Media Luna, or the Tortoise Reserve itself—are anywhere from 30 minutes to more than an hour (by car) from Puerto Ayora. The hikes can last from a few minutes to several hours.

Tortoise Reserve

Visiting the Tortoise Reserve can be quite a trek, but it's worth the effort. Visits there are limited to tour groups to protect the area. The walk to the reserve is gently rolling at first, then descends gradually. The path is very easy to follow. There are several things to notice along the way. One is the vegetation, which is typical of the rich, humid scalesia zone. The trees are much more leafy than the spare Palo Santo seen in the drier, lower areas. Their bark is covered with lichen and tufts of moss. Look for the thin umbrella shapes of the scalesia.

As you approach the fencing for the reserve boundary, see how strikingly different the agricultural land is from the reserve land. On one side of the trail is the agricultural land, which has banana or papaya plantations or has been cleared in places for cattle pasturage. On the other side of the trail is the richness of land left somewhat on its own. Seeing these contrasts can help the visitor understand how dramatic an effect human settlement can have on a fragile place such as this. It also points out the close relationship between competing claims for land use in the islands.

Birdwatching is excellent in this area. Both the large-billed and vermilion flycatchers can be seen. It is often overcast and shady along the trail, and that can make photography frustrating, but a fast film will reap rewards. (It is always a mystery to me why the vermilion flycatchers seem to spend most of their time on the lowest branch of the most shady tree—when they are near enough to photograph, anyway.)

But I have had special opportunities for once-in-a-lifetime shots, such as the vermilion flycatcher framed by wisps of gray moss and another one sitting on the great domed back of a tortoise, snapping at the insects that the tortoise stirred up.

Short-eared owls can be seen here, but I missed them. And the bird guidebook says that in rainy periods there are short-lived ponds where the white-cheeked pin-tail and both rail species can be seen.

But the tortoises put the capstone on this walk. Even before reaching the actual reserve boundaries, you are likely to start coming across the giant, dome-backed tortoise characteristic of Santa Cruz. It seems that they like to stick to the paths as much as the humans do, especially if it's muddy.

Seeing these beasts is unforgettable. On one trip, I looked for them eagerly; suddenly, there was a tortoise, and then another in a few minutes. They were a little taller than the bushes and at first I saw just the tops of their backs. And as I got closer they made a hissing noise. They pulled in their heads and feet, and as they did this I heard the sound of air being pressed out, as from a bellows, a puffing sound with little whistling overtones. Even when they shifted their heads as they fed, they puffed. It's a very soft and pleasant sound.

The chances of sighting tortoises may vary by the season, with encounters more likely in the more moist and cool times (roughly June to December). To ensure a comfortable trip, bring a light rain jacket (the kind that folds into its own pocket is ideal) or windbreaker because it can get fairly damp and chilly at these elevations. Lightweight slacks or heavier walking shorts should be adequate, and sturdy shoes that you don't mind getting damp and filthy also are a good idea.

Media Luna

The trip to Media Luna, a half-moon–shaped volcanic cinder cone, is less strenuous than the Tortoise Reserve hike. It is about an hour each way along an easy-to-follow, gently ascending path. Heavy mists are common, so a rain jacket is a definite asset.

To get to Media Luna you will be driven up to the settlement of Bella Vista, 7 kilometers from town. First the trail passes through the agricultural zone, and there are avocado and papaya groves, with wild guava bushes in abundance. As you continue up the gentle slope, the walk offers much the same scenery as the early part of the Tortoise Reserve hike; there are miconia plants and also the grassy pampa (fern and sedge) zone vegetation. There is a particularly good opportunity to see the miconia and the giant ferns there. They tower overhead and it is almost eerie to look up to a fern and see that its delicate fiddlehead is so large.

The birdwatching is good along the path, with a likelihood of seeing the wood-pecker and large tree finches. The birding guidebook says that at the higher levels, the upper limit of the miconia zone, the Galapagos rail can be heard and that a little lower down the paint-billed crake (Neocrex erythrops) can be found. Hawaiian pe-trels (Pterodroma phaeopygia) also nest in this area but are severely hampered in their nesting success by the predations of feral animals. Efforts to assess and improve the situation have been meeting with considerable success. As of 1999, the hatching success rate was 90 percent.

On clear days, a visit to Media Luna is very rewarding; the view extends all the way down the sloping side of Santa Cruz to Puerto Ayora. After a number of days on a boat, going from one and place to another, spending most time at sea level, this sweep of lush forest, grassland, and the turquoise harbor of the port is most refreshing.

Lava Tubes

Although these tubes are not an official park visitation site, they are certainly distinctive and interesting. Again, the guide makes arrangements to reach the location, which is off a side road from Bella Vista. There is a modest home near the beginning of the path and someone comes out to collect a very small entrance fee.

After a brief walk, you will encounter a big hole in the ground that forms a tunnel stretching beyond sight below and forward. The actual descent into the tube is just a scramble down some large rocks. A steadying hand from a friend probably is all the help you'll need. Then after a few meters the light begins to disappear, so bringing a flashlight is important.

The lava tubes were formed by rushing rivers of lava. Their outer surface cooled more quickly than the contents in the interior of the flowing mass, so the outer surface hardened sooner. The inner part continued to flow until it emptied itself onto the earth; thus, a hollow tube was left behind. There are actually two tubes here, the first curving down and then up to surface level. After a few meters on the surface you descend again into the second tube. Part of the roof of one of the tubes

View into a lava tube in the Highlands

caved in, and the hole, a couple of meters in diameter, admits light. The other tube is thoroughly dark. With or without a flashlight, walking in the tubes is quite easy. There's just the occasional rock or boulder to go over or around.

The tubes are the length of several buses and about three stories (10 to 15 meters) high. The walls are scored by the lava flow but otherwise straight and smooth. At the end of the last tube there is a makeshift handrail to help visitors climb out. When I was there, the exit was lovely as the light filtered back into the tube entrance, illuminating the greenery at the surface and highlighting the ferns that grew down into the tunnel.

There are other lava tube options for visitors—check with your guide about whether these may be part of your trip.

Los Gemelos

Los Gemelos ("the twins") are two pit craters, sections of the earth's surface that have fallen in on themselves as a result of movements of the earth's crust. At one time there was a layer of lava at the surface; when volcanic action below opened up an underground bubble, the surface collapsed onto itself, creating several acres of pit craters. Over time, vegetation has clothed the slopes of these depressions and the visitor sees a rich bowl of greenery.

Los Gemelos are located on either side of the road that goes between Puerto Ayora and Baltra, just 11 kilometers out of the port. It is a common destination for groups on their day in town. The site is an attractive one, just a few minutes' walk into the open area, which is in the scalesia forest zone and is rich in bird and plant life. The large-billed and vermilion flycatchers can be seen, and if you're lucky a short-eared owl may be perched on one of the moss-covered scalesia branches.

Caleta Tortuga Negra

This is "black turtle cove," a tidal lagoon that is almost mazelike in its complex shape. It is etched into the north coast of Santa Cruz, just southwest of Baltra. The cove has a narrow entrance, reached after a brief *panga* ride, and then it stretches nearly a kilometer inland and at its farthest end is more than half a kilometer wide. You will stay in your *panga* the whole time; after you have motored into the lagoon, your guide will cut the motor and just paddle quietly so that you can get the most out of the visit.

The entrance into the lagoon is a very good place to see all three kinds of mangrove plant: the red *(Rhizophora mangle)*, white *(Laguncularia racemosa)*, and black *(Avicennia germinans)*. Your guide will tell you how to distinguish one from the other.

Here you can see very clearly the role mangroves play in providing habitat for a wide variety of wildlife. Oysters cling to the roots, pelicans perch on their heights, and herons pick their way along the prop roots that link the branches to the muddy bottom. Mullet flash in and out of the fingerlike roots underwater.

Tortoises mating in the "black turtle cove"

Once you are well into the lagoon you are likely to be in for some very exciting moments. The brackish, calm waters are frequented by the white-tipped shark and rays of the spotted eagle and mustard (or "golden") varieties. Each time I have been there I have seen a number of the sharks, sliding below the boat or gathering in the shadow of the overhanging mangrove branches.

The rays are also an intriguing feature. The spotted eagle rays are easily a meter wide. They seem to hover at the surface and even raise their "heads" out of the water now and then.

The mustard rays are smaller, and when I saw them they were traveling in groups. They are very graceful, with the smooth movement of their "wings" showing alternately the cream-colored underside and the dull mustard color of their backs. They are diamond shaped, and they were traveling in diamond-shaped formation. The pattern-within-a-pattern of their movement was lovely.

You might see the green Pacific marine turtle here, for they gather here to mate. On one of my trips we were sitting quietly in the *panga*, when suddenly we heard a puff, a gentle moist exhalation behind us. We turned and saw the beak of a turtle just rising from the surface of the water. Then there was another puff a few meters in the other direction, then another and another. Next we noticed the water roiling not far away. We went a bit closer, and sure enough, the back of a turtle showed, then a flipper appeared, then the paler belly and another side and back. It became obvious that this was a pair of turtles locked into a copulatory embrace. They do this for hours, gently rolling, sometimes entirely submerged, sometimes both heads appearing as they come up for air.

The experience of this lagoon brought our group of very diverse people very close together. A sense of peaceful, smiling affection permeated the *panga* as we returned to our home boat and was sustained throughout the trip. It was not what we had come to the islands for, but it was an enjoyable result of the trip, just the same.

NEARBY SITES: PLAZA SUR, SANTA FE, MOSQUERA, DAPHNE MAJOR, SEYMOUR NORTE

Plaza Sur

Plaza Sur is a small island, the southern one of a pair of crescent-shaped islands not far off the east side of Santa Cruz. Plaza Sur is only 130 meters wide and a kilometer long. Unlike the conical volcanic islands, it is the result of shifts in the earth's crust, which have lifted it above the surface of the water. It is like a tilted tabletop, rising gradually from the beach to cliffs of about 20 meters on the south side.

Landing on the islands usually is easy because where it is necessary there will be a small cement jetty to which the *panga* can pull up. If the water is calm, you should be able to make a dry, sometimes slippery landing and then take the easy walk of about 1 hour. The only obstacle to landing (a temporary one) is that sea lions also love to lie on the jetty. If they really won't move at the arrival of visitors, then the guide may have to clap or make other noises to make them depart, which the sea lions do, in what seems to me to be a rather grumpy manner.

Once on the island, the first thing you'll notice is the vegetation. This is one of the islands with tree-sized opuntia, or prickly pear cactus *(Opuntia echios)*. They are very handsome with their bright russet bark, textured in a mosaic of elongated diamond-shaped plates. Rising from the bark are veritable explosions of gray spines, more than 3 centimeters long. Along the branches and at their tips are great fleshy paddles. These green paddles are a source of food for the finches and the land iguanas *(Conolophus subcristatus)* that are common here. It is wonderful to see the

Land iguana snacking

sturdy, pink-tongued iguanas stand on their hind legs to munch on those spine-laden pads. Leathery gums seem to be their savior.

I have been to Plaza Sur in an El Niño year, when the vegetation was at least knee-high and very green. The portulaca *(Portulaca oleracea)* was in splendid bloom, with the yellow flowers matching the brightest yellow hues of the land iguanas, which, from a distance, stood out from the greenery like overgrown flowers themselves.

But the more typical condition of extreme dryness prevails most years, and swaths of gray, rootlike vegetation are matted across the ground. In great contrast to the drab background is the brilliant rose-red of the *Sesuvium* plant, a colonizer of harsh sandy zones near the water. There are two species, which your guide can distinguish for you, that are endemic to the islands.

The sesuvium has fleshy branches, as many arid zone plants do. That is, they are a succulent, and like cacti they can hoard moisture in their fleshy parts, which are covered by a waxy exterior that retards moisture loss.

The path forms a circle in the middle of the island, running south overland, then east along the bluffs, back across the island, and then along the lower, boulder-strewn north shore. The trail is a classic example of park trail design, unobtrusively marked by the little gnarled posts of local wood, painted with a band of white and black. The trail is easy to follow and it goes exactly where you would want to go. As you begin the trek to the bluffs, there is a gradual incline. The sea lions are left behind and the light yellow and gray-green land iguanas begin to appear more frequently.

Soon the path comes closer to the black, rocky cliffs. Sheer in places, crumbly in others (exercise caution here), the cliff edge is a great place for birdwatching and sea watching. Swallow-tailed gulls *(Creagrus furcatus)* usually are there, with mottled gray and white young dotted along the cliffside and the adults wheeling and swooping in the incessant wind. (A windbreaker is useful here.) As they land against the air currents, there is usually a good opportunity to photograph them, wings outstretched, forked tails spread.

Not landing but often very common are red-billed tropicbirds *(Phaethon aethereus)* circling the island. There will be blue-footed and Nazca boobies, some perched on the cliff face. Hundreds of Galapagos shearwaters *(Puffinus subalaris)* may be swirling over the water's surface below. Frigate birds are ever present.

The cliff edge is a good place for spotting sea life as well. Two out of my five visits we spotted manta rays as big as a coffee table, cruising like underwater sailing ships just under the surface of the water. Once a hammerhead shark gave us a thrill, swimming below. (The hammerhead is so common in the islands that it has become the marine totem for the park.) There were also shoals of mullet devouring the same plankton the mantas feed on.

On the final quarter of the walk the trail traces the lower side of the island. First, near the water, are some small sandy areas lined with rocks. Marine iguanas bask and bob their heads in the sun. Continuing on, there is even less vegetation and a lot of

Blue-footed booby on its gravel nesting scrape

rocks and boulders to pick your way through. The rocks have a shiny white patina, the result of sea lion bodies polishing their own excrement year after year as they lumber over their territory to and from the water. Watch your step on these polished surfaces.

Plaza Sur is one of the few islands that have been spared the ravages of introduced species or uncontrolled human use. Other than goats and mice, there have been no introduced animal species, and the goats were eliminated by 1961. It is a good way to see what an island can be like: dense with wildlife, its natural plants intact, its spare beauty surrounding the visitor and the inhabitants alike. However, the heavy visitor use is taking its toll, and Plaza Sur has been taken off the list of sites that can be visited by large cruise ships. On the other hand, there are places only the large vessels can reach in a fairly short visit, and so this is all part of the Park's efforts to distribute visitor use in a fair way, so that everyone's chance to see a good variety of sites can be maximized—while wear and tear on the sites can be minimized.

Santa Fe

Santa Fe includes one of the few rigorous trail segments at the frequently visited sites. But it also has one of the most sheltered and beautiful anchorages of all the ones you will stay in. This deeply indented cove is marvelous for a quiet rest and swim after the slog up the cliff to see the land iguana species *(Conolophus pallidus)* that is unique to this island.

Santa Fe is 17 nautical miles from the southeast edge of Santa Cruz. Your boat ride will take from 1.5 to 3 hours, depending on its speed. Santa Fe is another uplifted island. It does have traces of surface volcanic activity, however. There are remains of underwater lava flows that were uplifted as the whole island plate was pushed to the surface.

After a wet landing on a small sandy beach, the group probably will be taken up

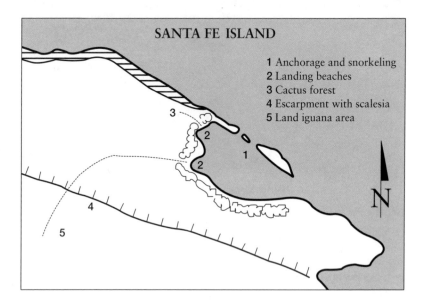

SANTA FE ISLAND

1 Anchorage and snorkeling
2 Landing beaches
3 Cactus forest
4 Escarpment with scalesia
5 Land iguana area

to the top of a distant cliff on your left. You will be looking for the land iguanas, which tend to frequent certain areas. Your guide will point these out.

The trail ascends gently at first, but at the base of the cliff there is perhaps 5 minutes' worth of steep ascent. The path is clear—there's nowhere else to go— but it can be crumbly and a little tiring if the temperature is already high. A helping hand from the guide or other visitors is all that's needed to reach the top.

On the way up, notice the huge opuntias here and the scalesia plants at the upper levels. Although scalesia is associated most often with the moist uplands, there are 14 species, several of which occupy the arid coastal zones. (The species seen here is *Scalesia helleri.*) You may notice that some of the plants on the steep slope have been tagged so that scientists can trace their development.

The trek to the top of the escarpment isn't always rewarded with an iguana sighting, but it is pretty common to see them there. This species is distinguished by its unusually heavy ridge of spikes along its backbone, rather like extremely tough, pointed fingernails. They can move briskly, although those I saw were deeply attached to the warm earth and the only movements evident were light breathing and the occasional eye blink.

Once you've made the trek to the escarpment and returned to the beach area, there may be time to take the short, low trail in the opposite direction. It goes to a very fine stand of opuntias *(Opuntia echios).* The brief walk is made more interesting by having to sidestep the usual group of sea lions that are lolling on the beach and in the shade of nearby rocks. En route to the opuntia forest our group had a rare sighting of a Galapagos snake—a sighting made even more unusual by the fact that it was ingesting a lava lizard headfirst, with half the lizard inside the snake and half out.

After you return to your boat, you will have a chance to enjoy the other highlight of Santa Fe: its beautiful cove. A long arm of rocks stretches from the beach and ends in a small island. You will be situated about halfway along the arm, enfolded by it. First check out the island itself for Galapagos hawks. They are regulars here. Once at night we were visited by an owl, which landed momentarily in our rigging. Pelicans are likely to be hovering around, and frigate birds will be attracted by the boat.

Looking up at the colorful cliffs on Sante Fe

But this is a place to be at one with the water. In such a protected cove, swimming is easy and snorkeling is good all along the inside of the rocky arm. You'll be joined by sea lions and other creatures as well.

Santa Fe was once plagued by goats, but they were eradicated in 1971. Thus what the visitor sees is an island well on its way to recovery. It's good to know that such distinctive beauty has a real chance to continue on its natural course.

Mosquera

Mosquera is a playground of sand, rocks, and tidepools. Sea lions have taken over the island, lolling around, sunning, and swimming. Their numbers have caused the Park to close the island to visitors.

The best view of Mosquera comes just as the plane is turning for its final descent to the Baltra runway. Look for the gleaming curve of white sand; that's Mosquera

Mosquera beach

flashing below you.

Birdwatching is good, even if it is from a panga. Pelicans and boobies post themselves on the higher rocks, and shorebirds peck and probe at the water's edge. I saw three semi-palmated plovers *(Charadrius semipalmatus)* and a sanderling *(Crocethia alba)*, two old friends from the north.

As you view the island from a boat, you can still feel how the heat and glare from the sand are moderated by the breeze. You may see one of the jet planes hurtling over you, and you'll feel lucky to be where you are, well into your visit to the Enchanted Islands.

Daphne Major

A visit to Daphne Major is an uncommon privilege, because of the wear and tear to its trails. There is a limit to how many times it can be visited by any given boat. Check with your captain as to whether your group will be visiting this tiny island.

Daphne Major is a small volcanic cone rising abruptly out of the sea just north of Santa Cruz and west of Baltra, and it is a frequently seen landmark. But its fragility and value to basic research on its varied birdlife have caused it to be set aside by the park, largely for scientific use. (Daphne Minor is a much smaller sibling of Daphne Major, just 6 kilometers north of it. Daphne Minor is only 0.08 square kilometer in area, one-fourth the size of Daphne Major.)

Daphne Major is slightly oval in shape, but from almost any direction at sea level it looks like a completely circular cone that has been lopped off crisply at the top. The landing is on its south side. Some consider the athletic leap and scramble from boat to land as one of the most difficult landings on the trip. Once on land, there are a few rocks to surmount and then a narrow, smooth path that winds gently upward to the crater rim, a walk of about 350 meters one way.

This is another site where you have to watch your step because the path is often occupied by nesting blue-footed boobies. (It's their home, after all.) This is a wonderful chance to compare the female and male blue-footed boobies. The females look as if they have a much larger pupil in their eye, a dark center surrounded by a thin ring of gold. Conversely, the males have a very small dark center in their eyes. (It is not a difference in pupil size, actually, but a difference in the degree to which the dark coloration of the iris extends over the yellow-colored part.) There is also a definite difference in their voices: The males have a high whistle and the females a much deeper tone, somewhat of a squawk. The females tend to be larger than the males, but because their plumage is so similar, it can be hard to make quick distinctions based on estimates of relative size. One of the best places to see them up close and to photograph them is near the summit of the trail. If you look at the rocky outcroppings, the scattered clusters of boulders, you are likely to see the Nazca booby at its nest.

Once you reach the rim of the crater you are in for a spectacular view in both directions: down into the crater and out to sea. The crater itself has two layers: a small flat circle not far below where the trail ends and another layer much lower. The lower level is much larger than the upper one, and your binoculars will help you get a detailed view of the nesting activity going on there.

The blue-footed boobies nest on the bright white floors of the crater. When I was there the nesting was not extensive, but there were still dozens of nests, which look like scrapes on the ground with bits of debris placed around their periphery. The occupied nests had large young, some showing only bright white fluffy down and others already having some of the dark brown of adult wing feathers. (The nests on the outer edge of the cone seemed less far along; most of the young were very recently hatched, with almost no feathers showing or very minimal down development.)

There was an ominous aspect to the scene below, however, as we saw a number of frigate birds patrolling the crater watching for any vulnerable young. It seemed that these young in the crater were too large to be taken easily; although they were sitting alone, they were not attacked. (The smaller ones near us seemed to be guarded by an adult at all times.) The frigate birds cruised, hovered a moment over a nest, and then cruised on, casting giant shadows on the birds below them. Then they ascended, often to the edge of the rim, circled it for awhile, and then went below again or out to sea.

At one point I was standing on the rim, changing film and looking down at what I was doing. Suddenly I felt an impact of air, almost like a wave, coming from behind me. I looked up, and rocketing overhead, very close, was one of the frigates. I had felt the wall of air it must have been pushing ahead of it. And I could see every feather distinctly, some raised, some lowered, like a huge collection of flaps stuck to an airplane's wing. Even though it was soaring, not flapping its wings, the flight was the most active thing imaginable. It was working the wind, clawing its way through it; there was nothing passive or gliding about it.

Another bird that you may well see from the crater rim, either flying around the perimeter of the cone on the ocean side or spiraling upward from the inner walls of the crater, is the red-billed tropicbird *(Phaethon aethereus)*. They aren't often seen at sea, so a place like Daphne Major where they nest in crevices in the rock provides one of the few dependable opportunities to see them. One may be sitting on a branch of the scrubby growth inside the crater, or you may see a tail sticking out of a hole among a pile of rocks that conceal its nesting place. And their straight, rapid flight, tail streaming, is a treat to see. It is possible to photograph them in flight if you're patient enough and quick enough with your camera. You'll probably want to use your telephoto lens for these flight shots. They'll be close, but not right on top of you. Afternoons seem to be a particularly good time to find a number of these birds in the area.

Much less obvious but very important to the birdwatcher are the finches of Daphne. Teams of ornithologists have been studying them for nearly three decades. (Do an Internet search for the work of ornithologists Peter and Rosemary Grant to trace the longest-running field research project ever done.) This is one of the few places where birds have been banded, so it is possible to trace the life histories of individual birds over the years. Invaluable knowledge about their breeding habits, their feeding patterns, and the effects of rain or drought on their survival rates has been collected. Sometimes there are scientists there, and it's a good chance to get a little more information about the birds and to find out what it's like to live for months on one small and very dry volcanic cone in the middle of the Pacific Ocean.

Seymour Norte

Seymour Norte is a very busy island. Its location puts it in the path of every boat. The large boats and even day trippers from Puerto Ayora are allowed to visit here. (In fact, Baltra is the current name for South Seymour, as Seymour Norte's sister island used to be known.) But it's also a busy nesting place of blue-footed boobies and the Galapagos' largest nesting colony of magnificent frigate birds *(Fregata magnificens)*. There are sea lions and swallow-tailed gulls, and maybe you'll even spot a Galapagos snake, as we did on one trip. And although it is not very dramatic, there is a distinct geological difference between this island and many of the others in the archipelago.

The island was formed by uplift of its rocky base from below sea level rather than

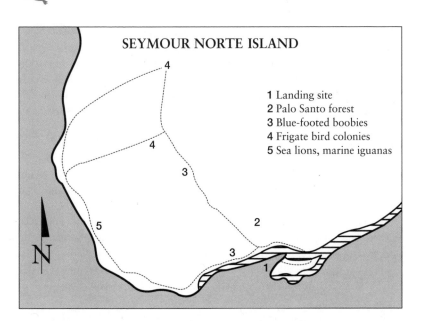

by the accumulation of lava and other debris that has formed the characteristically cone-shaped islands that make up most of the Galapagos. This kind of uplifting of the earth's crust, sometimes bringing the sea bottom high enough that it becomes dry land, is not uncommon in the islands. However, it is not the primary means of land building, even though all of the islands are made up of volcanic materials. But here the uplift of some ancient lava flow (formerly under water) has resulted in terrain that is fairly flat, often with a gentle slope in one particular direction. On Seymour Norte, the slope falls gradually away from the southern side with the low cliffs that greet the visitor at the landing site.

On my latest visit, the guide took the *panga* 100 meters or so along the face of the cliffs before we were taken to disembark. This was a very rich wildlife adventure. We saw how the swallow-tailed gulls occupy the rocky edges, waiting for night and their time to feed; got a close view of the many sea lions, with their young ones lounging in the tidepools; and saw great views of the black, polygonal columns of rock that form the cliffs.

The landing sometimes is difficult, depending on the size of the ocean swell. It's a short leap, aided by a crew member, onto a landing jetty. The one frustration at the landing point may be that, right there, you might see some swallow-tailed gulls. (They like rock-strewn cliffs, and these low ones have a certain appeal.) Then you may be torn between trying to watch your footing, not holding up anyone behind you, and trying to take some pictures very quickly. (You'll probably get a more leisurely look at them on Plaza Sur.)

At first glance, this is one of the most nondescript islands to be visited. However, the variety of Palo Santo that is found on Seymour Norte and Daphne *(Bursera malacophylla)* is endemic to those two islands. It is hairier and more stunted in appearance than its taller relatives on the other islands. Otherwise, you'll see flat ground, gray saltbush of uniform height, and some slightly more open areas with white-splashed rocks. At the beach area there may be young sea lions resting in what shade they can find.

Then, nearly at your feet, you may see your first blue-footed booby at its nest, cocking its golden eye at you, with perhaps a couple of eggs showing beneath it. Or maybe you'll see an ugly, gray, naked bag of avian entrails under a shading wing. (It's the whole chick, but in their earliest days they seem to be made mostly of bulbous gut and knife-edge beak.)

If there is nesting going on, you will almost certainly be treated to some fantastic displays. The blue feet play a major role in choosing a mate, setting up the nest, leaving that nest to feed or loaf, and returning to it without setting off antagonism or fear. They dip and bow, spread their wings, turn and twist them, and paddle the feet to show them off to best advantage. Lots of whistling and squawking go on as well.

It's not only the adults that do this, either. I have seen young still clothed in down, with only their wings fully feathered, engage in the same types of bowing, wing spreading, and tail tipping. Is it practice for the future or just avian fun?

It will be hard to move on from there, even though the birds are nearly oblivious

Young booby displaying or begging for food

to you, but there's a lot more to follow, for in a few minutes you come to the nesting grounds of the magnificent frigate bird.

A few great frigate birds nest there as well. This large and aggressive bird is a klepto-parasite, living off of the work of other birds, stealing their catch from them after vigorous chases in the sky. They have a wingspan of more than 2 meters and they are consummate flyers. In fact, it is hard to believe that a bird that big can be so quick on its wings.

Both the great and the magnificent frigate birds engage in this behavior, but the ones nesting on Seymour Norte are the latter. The females have white going all the way up their front to their chins. The field guide to the birds of the islands says that the males have a purple sheen to their plumage, particularly on the head (as opposed to a green sheen on the male great frigate birds). However, it can be pretty hard to distinguish between them in the field. But don't worry about the identification here because the birds themselves can tell very well, and so can your guide.

These huge birds build their scruffy nests on the tops of bushes at the farthest extent of the trail (which in its total length, a loop, is only slightly more than a kilometer long). If a male does not have a mate yet, he will sit on a nest and watch the females wheeling over. As one comes close overhead he may throw out his wings to their fullest extent, throw back his head, puff out his garish red throat pouch, and shake himself in a frenzy of invitation. However, once a pair has established themselves, whichever one of them is at the nest sits there quietly for the most part, particularly if they already have an egg or chick to care for.

The incongruities are great in this place: The huge dark birds, with their rapacious feeding habits and spectacular flying skills, sit quietly on low bushes, brooding or feeding young that, except for their long hook-tipped bills, look like they will never grow up to be what their parents are. They are a brilliant fluffy white until they are nearly the size of the parents. It takes months of careful nurturing for them to look and act like the patient adult birds that care for them.

To photograph the frigate birds, it is a good idea to bring a moderate telephoto lens as well as a standard one. The birds are big and not far away, but the nesting grounds are extensive and not all sites are occupied at any one time. Therefore, the bird that interests you photographically can be 10 or 15 meters away.

The trail also takes you along a narrow strip of pure white sand on the lower edge of the island. The sand wends its way between the more inland vegetation and the shoreline rocks. The walk is short here but very beautiful. You can go to the rocks and pools where the sea lions are or stay on the sand. Then you turn into the trail that goes into vegetation.

On your way out, if you have been going counterclockwise on the trail, you will be near the cliffs again. Along the beach itself there may be sea lions, and in the bushes near the shore there could be a Galapagos snake. The one we saw was about 2.5 centimeters in diameter and about a meter long. Like all other snakes on the islands, it was harmless.

Welcoming yellow-crowned night heron at fur seal grottos

3

Santiago and Nearby Sites

S antiago's numerous visitor sites and its location in the center of the islands make it one of the most familiar islands of a Galapagos tour. You go from site to site on Santiago, learning about the human history of the islands and seeing the fur seals or Galapagos hawks. Some of the shoreline was created by lava flows just a hundred years or so ago. You will take a quick jaunt to Bartolome's Pinnacle Rock or pull into the quiet cove of Sombrero Chino to anchor in a storm. But wherever you go around the island, the cone of Santiago's Sugarloaf Volcano or the sweep of black volcanic rock on its shores will appear again and again, giving you a visual anchor for a major part of your visit.

Santiago also may be the jumping-off point for the very long trip northeast to Genovesa, home of the red-footed boobies and thousands of storm petrels. It is also an important example of successful eradication of introduced species—with pigs eradicated in 2001 and the goat population eliminated in 2006.

Goat skeletal remains on Santiago

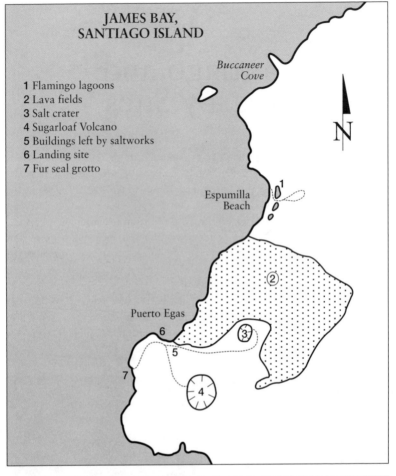

**JAMES BAY,
SANTIAGO ISLAND**

1 Flamingo lagoons
2 Lava fields
3 Salt crater
4 Sugarloaf Volcano
5 Buildings left by saltworks
6 Landing site
7 Fur seal grotto

Buccaneer
Cove

Espumilla
Beach

Puerto Egas

N

SANTIAGO (SAN SALVADOR, JAMES)

Your itinerary is likely to bring you back to Santiago (James) Island several times. Its visitor sites are on the east and west sides of the island, and its central location in the archipelago means that your route will pass it often as you criss-cross to the more distant islands or to the numerous visitor sites on nearby islands.

This island has powerful evocations of past human use, although with eradication of goats complete, it is now recovering from this scourge, and also healing from several attempts at salt mining. It also has some of the most impressive natural sites: the fur seal grottos, a flamingo lagoon, and the geologically recent lava flows at Sullivan Bay. At each of the sites, birdwatching

Petrels feeding in an El Niño year

is particularly rewarding, with sightings of flamingos, Galapagos hawks, or vermilion flycatchers likely. Migrating shorebirds are seen regularly also.

James Bay

This bay, on the northeast side of Santiago, is a lovely stopping place in itself, but its chief function is the starting point for three visitor sites: the salt crater, the fur seal grottos, and Espumilla Beach, with its flamingo lagoon. The first two are reached from the same anchorage, and Espumilla Beach is a short boat ride to the northern end of the bay.

Before moving to the visitor sites themselves, it's worth noting that this bay usually offers a particularly good chance to savor the sea life around you. If you are there in the early morning or later afternoon, sit on deck and watch what goes on around the boat. The boobies plunge for fish, and the pelicans dive and then swim along the surface, followed closely by the brown noddies, who hope that fish will spill out of the pelicans' pouches. Sometimes a noddy even sits on a pelican's head to be really close to the action. Sally Lightfoot crabs scuttle over the exposed black rocks near the shoreline. (They're especially easy to see on the one rock protruding, fingerlike, above the surface near the point where you will disembark.)

When I was there in an El Niño year, this anchorage was the place where I saw the most storm petrels *(Oceanodroma castro)* at once, flitting and dipping over the water's surface as they fed. The water was so calm that in the flat light of evening it gleamed as though dark oil had been poured on it. Only these tiny birds, themselves nearly completely black, relieved the unbroken somberness as I peered down onto the water.

Puerto Egas and the Salt Crater

After a wet landing the visitor walks a few dozen meters to the area used until the 1960s as a port for a salt extraction operation, restarted decades ago by a Señor Egas. From this area the view is rather bleak: a collection of rusted hulks of old machinery and the remains of posts from defunct sheds.

The trail, which actually follows the remnants of a road wagons once used to haul the salt, starts to wind away from the shore and up around the slopes of the crater's cone. It's hard to get much of a sense of the topography at first; there's just a slope on your left side and flat ground to the immediate right. It's an easy walk, although on a very hot day it can seem a lot longer than it is. Wear tennis shoes, not sandals; light-weight slacks also are a good idea. Somehow this hike seems to be one of the hottest excursions. The way to minimize discomfort is to keep a close eye on the sights alongside as you walk, and don't be impatient to reach the rim of the salt crater itself.

But move along; as the elevation gradually increases, the birdwatchers in the group probably will have some great moments. The slope of the crater is a likely place to see the vermilion flycatcher *(Pyrocephalus rubinus)*. Just as it stands out in the dark

Overview of the abandoned salt pond

greenery of the highlands of Santa Cruz, this bird makes a stark and beautiful contrast here with the gray Palo Santo trees that clothe the slopes of Santiago. It will be sitting on a branch, head and chest red beyond imagining, and then it will launch itself out into the air to snap at an insect too small and too fast for a human eye to see. The click of its bill as it makes the catch is how you'll know he's succeeded (or she, if it is the more subtly colored buff-and-brown female). Then the bird circles back to its original perch, having completed a circle perhaps a meter in diameter.

With luck, you will see the large-billed flycatcher *(Myarchus magnirostris)*, too. Its colors are not as spectacular, but its similar feeding habits are just as interesting.

The trail usually is rich with finches. I saw the warbler finch here once, and the famous woodpecker finch, the dream of anyone interested in bird behavior. For me it happened as I noticed a bird that seemed to be pecking into a tree. I went closer, thinking, "Could *this* be the woodpecker finch?" As I got closer, I saw that it had a spine in its bill, a cactuslike spine, about an inch long. And it was using the spine to probe into the tree. I was completely amazed to actually see something that I'd read about and seen in films: how an animal uses a tool.

Then it dropped that spine and came back with a wobbly-looking one, crooked, with little wisps coming off it (not a spine, in other words). After the bird tried probing with it a couple of times, to no avail because it bent, it dropped that twig and went off to another tree that had thorns and picked one of those. That one seemed to work.

Another birding event can happen on this trail: an appearance of the Galapagos hawk at the end of the trail, just as you come out onto open ground at the rim of the crater. It can be quite windy there, and the hawks seem to like this place for tossing themselves around in the wind currents overhead—that is, when they're not sitting quietly on one of the nearby tree branches staring down at the visitors.

At the rim of the salt crater are marvelous sights on both sides. First is the crater itself. Its volcano is long extinct, and its floor is about 10 meters below sea level. Evidently salt water seeps in slowly through cracks in the rock; as it comes up in the crater itself, a shallow, briny lake is formed. The fierce sun evaporates the surface water and the remains can be collected as usable salt. Several efforts have been made to create a viable business of this, one as late as the 1960s, but none succeeded. (Of course, such an enterprise would be prohibited in today's national park.)

It's possible at times to see remains of impoundments that were made for drying the salt further. The remains of these still cut the circular lake into pie-shaped wedges. The edges usually are a brilliant white, and the center may be white, tan, or bright green, depending on the water level and the growth of algae. Look closely for a flamingo or two in the distance; you may be lucky.

You will be seeing here a scene that Darwin described in his *Voyage of the Beagle*. He reported,

One day we accompanied a party of the Spaniards in their whale-boat to a

Salina, or lake from which salt is procured. After landing, we had a very rough walk over a rugged field of recent lava, which has almost surrounded a tuff-crater, at the bottom of which the salt-lake lies. [Obviously, he took a different route than the modern visitor takes.]

The water is only three or four inches deep, and rests on a layer of beautifully crystallized, white salt. The lake is quite circular, and is fringed with a border of bright green succulent plants; the almost precipitous walls of the crater are clothed in wood, so that the scene was altogether both picturesque and curious. A few years since, the sailors belonging to a sealing vessel murdered their captain in this quiet spot, and we saw his skull lying among the bushes.

Today's visitor isn't allowed to go down into the crater to see whether the skull is still there or to see the salt crystals up close. You will see clearly from the rim, across the crater, the remains of the road that was constructed more recently to bring out the salt. Now it's just a pale gash, gracefully winding around half of the crater's interior slope.

If you turn in the other direction, looking directly away from the crater's center, you face wave upon wave of black and orange lava fields. These vast sweeps of earth of contrasting color very much characterize the vistas on the island. The older flows—the orange ones—have a fair amount of vegetation scattered over them. The stark gray of the Palo Santo trees is broadcast over the orange slopes as far as the eye can see. The more recent black flows seem utterly barren, and only a much closer examination allows the visitor to see that even here, plant and animal life exist.

The Fur Seal Grottos

The fur seal grottos are only a 763-meter walk from the same landing used for the salt craters. The level, sandy trail is off to the right, roughly following the edge of the island but a few meters in from the somewhat rocky shore. The trail here is very good for birdwatching. There may be Galapagos hawks; often there are shorebirds feeding on tidbits along the wave-splashed rocks.

On almost all of my visits I have seen oystercatchers *(Haematopus ostralegus)*, most impressive with their black and white plumage, red bill, yellow-ringed eye, and ugly pink feet. Three whimbrels flew overhead once, and finches are common in the nearby brush. It's worth checking any seaweed exposed along the shoreline to see whether the yellow warbler is feeding there. I saw them most often in these circumstances, their yellow showing up clearly against the green of the damp vegetation.

In places, the rocks are also packed with marine iguanas. Quite often they are piled on each other in layers, two or even three deep. This seems to be a way of retaining each other's body heat. They seem to compete with each other for the spot that has the most direct exposure to the sun, even if it means clinging nearly vertically from a shoreline boulder with tails hanging out into space.

The walk will be an easy 15 minutes, ending at a small plain of black lava flow. This area is pocked by three aquamarine potholes. These holes are formed in the same way that the Santa Cruz lava tubes were formed, only these are not land-locked. The lava flow went out to the open sea and now the water rushes in and out of the tubes with the tides. The tops have caved in here and there, making the open pothole that you look down into. At one time, visitors could swim in these grottoes, but the combination of risks to swimmers of surging tides and of disturbing the wildlife has closed this option.

The main two pools are a wonderful sight, however, connected as they are to each other, with a bridge of black lava arching over them near the middle of their length. The exit of the pool to the open sea also has an arch over it, where it's great just to sit and watch the water flow back and forth below you.

Basking fur seals at grottos

A young visitor in a quiet moment

You'll have company here. The fur seals will be lounging around at the edges of the pools. Seals will swish below with total ease and nonchalance.

The grottos are only about 15 meters long, but for sheer beauty and ease of access, few places on the island can compete with their black rocks, crystal clear blue water, fur seals, and tropical fish. Each time I was there, I saw what I like to think is the same yellow-crowned night heron on exactly the same rock, just a step below the rim of the largest pool. It was like some welcoming sign, confirming for the visitor that all was well.

Espumilla Beach

Espumilla Beach, at the northern shore of James Bay, has historic significance. Just north of it is a source of fresh water, much prized by pirates who plied these waters centuries ago. Now visitors go there for the quiet beach and birdlife in the vegetation lining the beach. I've seen common stilts and white-cheeked pintails there in the fresh water that sometimes collects behind the dunes.

A 2-kilometer trail goes inland from the beach. It makes a slight ascent over a knob of land and then loops back to its starting point. There are several finch species to see, and perhaps vermilion flycatchers.

Buccaneer Cove

Buccaneer Cove is less than an hour's sail north of James Bay and Espumilla Beach. It is not a visitor site as such, and your boat may just sail into the cove so your guide can tell you about its human history. That history is fascinating and important, but be sure to take a good look at the scenery; the cliff walls in particular are spectacular.

The cove served generations of pirates and then whalers as a safe harbor near one of the few freshwater sources in the islands. They would land, take on water, perhaps kill a few tortoises for fresh meat, and gather firewood for the ship's galley. Remains of ceramic vessels have been found submerged offshore; antilitter campaigns certainly had no meaning in those days.

Seeing the cove can give you a few vicarious chills at the thought of these men, living at the edges of human law and their own physical endurance. But it also can give you a very immediate sense of awe as you look up at the vast, vertical walls, especially on the north side, that encompass much of the cove. The cove is the remnant of a volcano that formed at the edge of the island. You can trace the layers upon layers of volcanic debris that have been deposited over time. Sometimes explosions expelled tons of fine materials, which settled back around the central vent and built up the walls of the crater. Other layers are composed of molten lava that pushed up more slowly and partially filled the crater's depths.

Wind, rain, and the invading ocean have eroded the cove walls to leave some of the most dramatic scenery in the islands. On the south wall in particular are the multihued strata that tell of the cone's growth and erosion. All along the north wall there are great pockmarks, caves, and fingerlike vertical protrusions. Here the wall's deep browns and ochres are splashed with the white of bird excrement, an undignified source of lovely visual accents. And frigate birds and boobies sit peering out to sea or launch themselves out for a fishing sortie. Your boat may come very close to the wall to give you a good view. The closeness may be a bit nerve-racking, but your guide probably will explain that the cliffs are as perpendicular below the surface as above and that the water there is very deep indeed. So be sure to be out on deck with binoculars and camera and be ready to take in these brief but spectacular moments.

Sullivan Bay: The Lava Flows

As your boat passes by Santiago on its various trips and as it pulls into Sullivan Bay itself, you often see wedges of black lava cutting across the island's reddish slopes. Santiago is a classic volcanic island, rising to a dominant cone nearly 1000 meters tall at its northwest side. It also has many smaller cones projecting from its major slope, some having craters and others not.

Sullivan Bay is the place to be reminded of how active the volcanic earth building is in the Galapagos. This site features a lava flow slightly more than 100 years old. It is a great swath of lava that oozed down to the sea, curling around small cones that came before it, adding land at the sea's edge where there was no land before. There is a lot to be learned here about land-building processes, but first there is the feeling of astonishment and mystery as you walk over the shiny black lava fields.

The landing is a dry one onto a small ledge. You should wear lightweight running shoes to protect your feet on landing and on the fairly smooth but sun-baked lava flow. (Your guide may have toughened bare feet, but visitors rarely do.) Watch for penguins near the landing area. You may be lucky.

As you enter the lava field, what looks from a distance to be monotonous

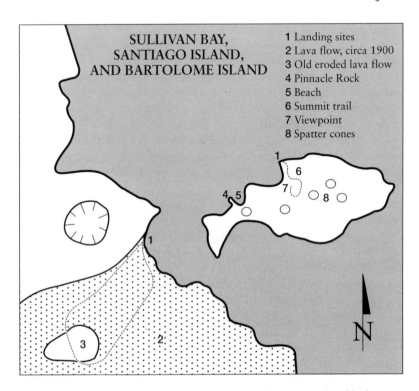

SULLIVAN BAY,
SANTIAGO ISLAND,
AND BARTOLOME ISLAND

1 Landing sites
2 Lava flow, circa 1900
3 Old eroded lava flow
4 Pinnacle Rock
5 Beach
6 Summit trail
7 Viewpoint
8 Spatter cones

N

paving turns out to be a multilevel terrain of sheer fascination. It is like being in immobile black batter—110 square kilometers of it. The proper name for this kind of flow is *pahoehoe*, pronounced with five syllables ("pa-**ho**-e-**ho**-e"). The word is Hawaiian for "ropey." It is used by scientists everywhere to describe the same type of lava flow and surface character. It is a very apt word, conveying very well the shapes the lava takes as it flows fairly slowly, hardening into fans and swirls and protrusions of roughly parallel rope-shaped strands.

This kind of pattern is formed when the superheated lava cools more rapidly on its surface than in its interior. The lower, hotter part continues to flow and the upper parts begin to drag as they cool and harden. This uneven cooling gives the flowing mass its characteristic fan shape, with a series of curving creases roughly perpendicular to the direction of the flow. The flatness of the land over which it flows (the lava tends to separate and flow around obstacles such as earlier-established volcanic cones) and the fact that this flow went rather slowly overall (it was not the result of explosive volcano-building) allowed the flow to meander.

There are fans a few inches in diameter as well as ones several meters across; they all interweave and overlap in the most marvelous fashion. Some of them look very much like other things; one part you're likely to see is the one called "pig guts" by the locals, and there's no arguing the accuracy. (Other names are more elegant, some less.)

There are various levels of this huge gleaming surface, evidently because of the buildup of gases below, which could raise a section and then let it drop as the gas cooled. There are some very large cracks where you can see down to other layers of rock; the average depth of the whole field is 2 meters. Some cracks take a bit of a jump to get across, or you can just follow the crack to its end and keep going in a slightly different direction.

Another intriguing part of this flow is the plant life, past and present. Where the flowing lava encountered a plant, especially a woody section of one, it flowed around and quickly vaporized the encased plant. However, in a few cases the plant lasted long enough to leave a clear imprint, sometimes completely in the round (or hollow) of its shape. There is something eerie about this quick immortalizing process.

The lava flow also is a lesson in plant colonization. The flow is so recent, the rock so hard, and the rainfall so scarce that there is almost no organic material, much less true soil. Yet plants are scattered here and there on the stark surface. The most obvious plant is a form of cactus called the lava cactus *(Brachycereus nesioticus)*. It looks like a fistful of very prickly cucumbers joined together at the base and then fanning outward and upward for 10 to 25 centimeters or so. The growing tips tend to be a bright straw color, with the older base being dark gray.

The other early colonizer of the nearly soil-less lava flow is the carpetweed plant

Newer black lava flow on older volcanic slope. Bartolome Pinnacle is in background.

(Mollugo flavescens). It forms a network of wispy stems that hug the surface of the lava and spread out only 15 or 20 centimeters. Sometimes its tiny flowers are visible.

If there is little plant life to be seen here, there is even less animal life. There may be the painted locust, and a very colorful grasshopper *(Schistocerca melanocera)*, but for the most part, flies and lava lizards are just about it, the latter preying on the former.

As you walk inland, it is possible to see what this flow may look like many thousands of years from now. At the edges of the black tongues of new lava there is soil, although it is very coarse. This soil has oxidized to a rich rust color. Plants have taken hold and there is sparse shrubbery, none of it very high. Take a walk out onto the older ground and look back at the lava. Think what it was like 100 or so years ago, to hear and smell and see that lava coming toward you. Was it fast, or would it have been easy to step out of its path and head for the safety of that low hillock? No one was there at the time, but someone might be next time.

BARTOLOME (BARTHOLOMEW)

This is the single most visited place in the Galapagos. If you saw just one photograph of the islands before you came, it probably was of Bartolome's Pinnacle Rock, towering over a perfect blue cove, lined by a copper-colored beach, and set off by the rugged profile of Santiago not far in the distance.

There are two sites on this small island: a hike up an extinct lava cone for a sweeping view of the nearby islands and a beach where snorkeling and birdwatching can be very good.

Summit Trail

The landing for the summit trail is a dry one, directly from the *panga* onto a rock and concrete stairway from water level. The trail is 600 meters one way. It is a wonderfully designed and sturdily constructed boardwalk, built to preserve the fragile tuff cone surface from the erosion of thousands of visitor feet. The boardwalk steps are easy to manage, wide and not too high. There are several points where you can pause and look out at the increasingly spectacular view as you make the ascent.

All along the walk, you will be struck by the stark beauty around you. The gracefulness of the contours contrasts with the near-barrenness of the slope on which you climb. As you look closer, you will see the little lava lizards scampering across the ground or sitting on one of the small boulders that were blasted out of the throat of the now-extinct volcano that formed the island.

Scattered at distant but regular intervals are wispy plants, spreading themselves out to maximize access to moisture. They serve an important function in these condi-

Pedestrian boardwalk on Bartolome protects the island's fragile surface

tions by stabilizing the ground in which they put down their roots. The two spreading ones are *Chamaesyce amplexicaulis,* which has greenish stems, and *Tiquilia nesiotica,* the more thinly spreading of the two, which has grayish stems. And you will see that early colonizer of sere surfaces, the lava cactus *(Brachycereus nesioticus).* It looks like a very spiny cucumber, darker near its roots and often yellow at the growing tip.

As you follow the path, you soon come to a number of spatter cones on both sides of the trail. These are very large intrusions of lava through the gravelly tuff

Early colonizer on slopes of Bartolome

slopes. Some of the cones are flat at the top, with minicraters within. Some rise up 5 or 10 meters, and one side has been stripped away. They are strikingly colored, with deep reds and iridescent blacks and deep greens blending into each other.

Near the top you can see that the island has dozens of these cones in various stages of erosion. There are lava tubes, too, in differing sizes and various states of preservation. They look like twisting tram lines from far above. Overall, the island can make you feel as if you are on the surface of the moon, with craters scattered in every direction. The water is so clear that you can see more cones submerged near the shore, and you realize that the bay is an underwater crater, somewhat larger than many of those dotting the land. The geology of this area is so fascinating and the scenery so stark that one of our party, a geologist, told us that this visit would be second only to a trip to Mars.

The wind picks up as you reach the very top of the island, so it's best to bring a windbreaker here. There are several flat areas on which to stand and look all around you. There is nowhere else on the islands where you can get such a strong sense of the sheer number and variety of sizes of the islands of the Galapagos. The nearest island you can see is Santiago, a few minutes away by boat. South are Santa Cruz, Baltra, and Seymour Norte. Rabida is to the southwest. And there are dozens of islets and large rocks protruding from the ocean's surface.

The larger islands are dramatically colored, with the typical orange base, the sweeps of black lava, and the fringes of gray plant life. The ocean's color ranges from nearly white at shorelines to turquoise to blue and gunmetal gray. The profiles of the land, the contours and dimensions, are endlessly fascinating and beautiful. Pinnacle Rock (about 70 meters high) at the mouth of the Bàrtolome cove sets off the scene admirably. The top of the island is very far above it, and you can easily see the frigate birds that use it as a roost between their raids on other birds.

Keep an eye on the water further out, too. On my latest visit, huge manta rays were leaping out of the water, turning somersaults as they emerged.

Naturally you'll want your camera. Polarizing filters are a must here so that you can choose whether you want the underwater craters to show. There is likely to be very strong glare, whether the day is clear or overcast. For portraying the scenery here, both a wide-angle and a normal lens are necessary. The wildlife is mostly lava lizards, so a 100- to 200-mm lens should do fine.

The Bartolome Beaches

When you make the easy but wet landing at the beach at Bartolome, you will be on the north side of a narrow neck of land that stretches between the larger section of the island—where you probably just climbed to the top—and the smaller section, from which Pinnacle Rock soars. From the shore there is a 100-meter walk to the beach on the far side. Of interest on the walk are the plants that take hold on the upper reaches of many Galapagos beaches: red and white mangrove, saltbush,

Top: Penguins at Bartolome (Photo by Helena Zukowski)

Center: Hawaiian petrel on the wing

Bottom: Nesting red-billed tropicbird on Plaza Sur

Left: Sesuvium on San Cristobal

Top: Striated rock jutting out into James Bay and landing for Puerto Egas and fur seal grottos

Center: Oystercatcher and sea urchin at grotto area tide pools (Photo by Ron Esson)

Bottom: Young fur seal; note tiny, low-set ears

Next page, top: Red-footed booby at Punta Pitt on San Cristobal

Bottom left: Great blue heron welcomes visitors to a restaurant's dock

Bottom right: Mustard rays at the edge of the mangrove roots at Caleta Tortuga Negra

Top: Overview of Bartolome's Pinnacle Rock and beaches with Sullivan Bay Lava Flow in the background (Photo by Helena Zukowski)

Above: Dragonfly on Santiago

Left: View from the boat

Top: Sante Fe land iguana

Left: Crew members
coming to pick up a group
from an island visit

Below: Cleft in the sand of
Mosquera's beach

Top: Young sea lion
sleeping on a mosaic of
white sand and dark
rock

Bottom: Powerful surge
of incoming tide at
grottos

Next page, top: Pelicans
on Rabida's russet
slopes

Center, top: Giant
tortoise in brilliant
greenery of the
Highlands

Center, bottom: Sea lion
pups play on Rabida's
orange sand beach

Bottom: Albratrosses
fencing

Right: Flamingo up
close

Right: Great frigate bird male on nest

Below: Capitan of a motor-sailing boat

Overview of Bartolome isthmus, looking toward Sullivan Bay lava flows

morning glory, and prickly pear. The path is not wide, but it is clear and you won't have to dodge too many spines or brushy slaps in the face.

On the south side you may see sea turtles if it is their nesting season. This is one of the beaches where they lay their eggs (January to March). You will be able to explore most of this beach. However, you are not allowed in the water, so that you won't disturb the variety of wildlife often found near the shore (sharks, turtles, various rays). Your guide will help you spot where turtles have laid eggs under the sand, and you will be able to go around them. Those turtles don't need any more problems with survival than they have already, so tread carefully.

There may be great blue herons stalking along the shoreline. It is also worthwhile to give a careful squint down into the water, for it is not uncommon to see hammerhead, black-tipped, and white-tipped sharks cruising the shallows.

Back at the north beach, you probably will have a chance to go swimming. The cove is an excellent spot for snorkeling; the submerged rocks and underwater ridges have a wide variety of undersea life. And you are still quite near shore and in fairly shallow water. Don't forget to look on the rocky shore near the Pinnacle for some penguins. There may be two or three and they are wonderful to see. If you aren't swimming, your guide may take you on a *panga* ride around the Pinnacle point, and you may see penguins along the rocks there or swimming nearby.

NEARBY SITES: SOMBRERO CHINO, RABIDA

Sombrero Chino

A visit to this small island is likely to be easygoing, comfortable, and surprisingly interesting. Sombrero Chino ("the Chinese hat") is just 200 meters away from the southeast coast of Santiago, not far from the Bainbridge Rocks. The island is nestled into a protective curve of Santiago's shore, and this creates a quiet channel for boats to anchor in. Your boat may stay there more than once because of the island's location on the crossroads between the much-visited islands of Santa Cruz and Santiago and because it is a refuge if the sea is stormy.

For the landing on Sombrero Chino, the *panga* will take you to a lovely crescent-shaped beach with bright white sand. It's a wet landing but not difficult. Right away you may be among sea lions, lolling as they do on the beach or on the sandy patches scattered along the rocky shore.

The trail is only about 350 meters long. It ends at a very rocky point where waves crash in a spectacular fashion. The path is close to the shore and is an easy walk, although sturdy shoes are a good idea because of the intermittent rockiness.

The volcanic origin of the island is very clear. There are the remains of several types of lava flow here and numerous small lava tubes, some only centimeters in diameter. Many are broken and rather rough to walk on. There are patches of *pahoehoe* lava, the smooth, ropey lava. It is very black and shiny. In tiny pockets that have accumulated a bit of soil, you will see one of the early colonizers of lava flows, the plant *Sesuvium edmonstonei*. Its leaves are thick and fleshy and look more like branching stems than the leaves on shrubs in moister environments. In the driest time of the year the leaves are a rose color that almost glows against the black rock. The stems hug the rock as they branch out 40 to 50 centimeters.

The shoreline has a number of rocky protrusions that are much loved by pelicans. You should have some great chances to photograph them. The shore itself is very rich. It teems with Sally Lightfoot crabs. How their brilliant oranges and blues stand out against the wet, black rocks!

On the inland side is the Sombrero itself, rising above you with its rust-red sides, punctuated by the light grays of the Palo Santo and of the more shrublike spreading *Tiquilia nesiotica*. The low light of early morning or late evening seems to bring out the best of the contrasting colors of rock and plant on the slopes of the now-silent volcano.

Rabida

At first glance, Rabida is another typical beach-plus-mangrove-plus-flamingo lagoon site. But what makes it very different and very memorable is the color of the beach and island soil: a rich russet that gleams in the sun and gives everything on it a special quality of soft beauty. The reddish hue comes from the oxidation of the iron-rich lava that is the basis of its soil.

The island is an hour and a half by boat from Sombrero Chino. It is small, just a little over 2 kilometers across at its widest point. It is steep and rugged and rises to more than 400 meters at its highest point, although the visitor will be staying at the lowest elevations. The chief vegetation on the slopes is opuntia cactus, Palo Santo

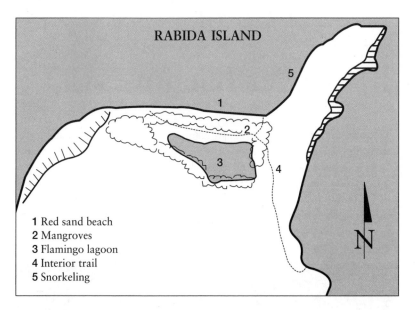

1 Red sand beach
2 Mangroves
3 Flamingo lagoon
4 Interior trail
5 Snorkeling

trees, and other scrubby bushes. Right at the shoreline is the band of mangrove that separates the beach from the saltwater lagoon inland just a few meters.

The landing is a wet one onto the narrow strip of beach. Usually a number of sea lions are on the beach or in the small caves that have been formed in the cliffs at the water's edges. Even if you see no sea lions basking or swimming at the beach, your nose will tell you whether they are still to be found a little farther on. Be careful when you walk into the mangrove strip because the sea lions also love to sleep in the shade of the bushes. It is entirely possible to unexpectedly step on an extended flipper. An irritated sea lion can move amazingly quickly and inflict quite a bite, so caution is called for.

It takes only a minute or two to reach the lagoon. With any luck there will be flamingos sieving through the brackish water for the minute plant and animal life that they depend on for food. Each time I was there we also saw several Galapagos white-cheeked pintail ducks *(Anas bahamensis)*. This is a very attractive bird with a steel-blue bill decorated by fuchsia stripes along its lower length.

The trail is a gentle 1-mile circular route. It goes up a slight slope to a cliff that overlooks a small ocean inlet. The path leads to an excellent view of a tiny cove; its white sandy bottom and blue waters are set in the frame of the red cliffs on which you stand. You will have a lovely stroll among the Palo Santo trees, and there are some sweeping views of the ocean from the low cliffs that the trail approaches. Always there is the contrast of red soil, blue water, white sea floor, and gray-green vegetation.

4
Tower (Genovesa)

Tower is a small island (10.5 square kilometers) at the upper right-hand corner of the Galapagos archipelago. It is not visited as often as the more central islands because of the length of the voyage and the possibility of rough seas. There are two visitor sites on the island: the beach and tidepool area around Darwin Bay and the inland area reached from the bay by what are known as Prince Philip's Steps. Both sites are particularly good for seeing interesting birdlife.

Red-footed booby chick

DARWIN BAY

After an easy wet landing there is a short walk up the brilliant white coral beach to a bizarre area of inland tidepools and rugged outcroppings of black rock several meters high. The greenery edging the pools is the saltbush *(Cryptocarpus pyriformis)*, or *monte salado,* as it is known in Spanish. These pools are feeding sites for shore-birds such as wandering tattlers, turnstones, whimbrels, and lava gulls (which nest in the cliffs of the island, as do swallow-tailed gulls). Yellow-crowned, lava, and black-crowned night herons are found there, too, although the latter are fairly rare.

Although warblers certainly are not considered shorebirds, it is common to see the yellow warbler probing along the edges of the tidepool for the little fiddler crabs and other minute shore life. (In fact, the majority of times I have seen the yellow warbler in the Galapagos, it has been right at the shoreline as it pecked and probed among the vegetation.)

Here or at other places on the island you may see lava gulls, which nest on the cliffs and the west side of the bay, and swallow-tailed gulls, which nest on the cliffs of the eastern side.

The trail follows the line of the bay until it reaches higher and more arid ground, but you may find yourself completely occupied by the birdlife you see first. When I was there we saw dozens of great frigate birds *(Fregata minor)* on nests and loafing on the rocks and shrubs. It was during a year of the heavy rain and severe heat of the El Niño current. The temperature on land that morning must have been at least 30°C. with nearly 100% humidity (and not raining). We could hardly keep walking; there was no breeze behind the huge boulders that lined that part of the bay.

The birds were suffering as well. Many of them were sitting in the most grotesque

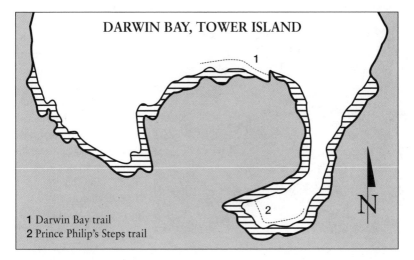

DARWIN BAY, TOWER ISLAND

1 Darwin Bay trail
2 Prince Philip's Steps trail

positions, apparently trying to maximize their cooling. Some sat hunched on a branch, heads drooping very far down on chests, wings turned with the underside out. Others sat on the nearly vertical sides of rocks, with heads up and tails spread out almost like shovels, and their wings were bent so that they looked like they had their "arms" akimbo, also exposing the inner lining of the wings.

Some of the birds were on nests, although there were no young in sight. Rather, the males seemed to be trying very hard to attract mates. This was where we got the best view of the display of their outspread wings, inflated pouch, and whinnying whistles as they tried to communicate with females flying overhead. With these huge birds and their contorted postures, the glaring of white sand and black rock, and the heat that seemed to be baking our brains, this visit had a nightmarish quality, as though we were on the edge of delirium. Even the water was too warm to offer real relief. You probably won't run into that kind of heat, but then the birds may not be doing such strange things, either. No two visits are alike; all are fascinating.

PRINCE PHILIP'S STEPS

The landing for this site is a dry one. The so-called steps actually are a steep 25-meter scramble up a cleft in the cliffs on the east side of Darwin Bay. They were given their name after a visit by Great Britain's Prince Philip in 1964.

Once you reach level ground, there is a wealth of varied birdlife. One of the first species you may see is the red-footed booby, which nests on the low bushes here. After seeing all those blue-footed and Nazca boobies nesting on the ground, it seems incongruous to see their treeborne counterparts perched above you, their garish red webbed feet curled over the branches they sit on. About 95 percent of the red-foots are a dark beige; the other 5 percent are white. Both plumage types are the same species.

Scattered over the island are nests of the Nazca booby, which use several kinds of terrain for nesting. In general, their breeding season lasts from September to July. They have elaborate and almost bizarre territorial, mate selection, and nest maintenance displays, rivaling those of their blue- and red-footed relatives.

Mockingbird

Short-eared owl

The scrubby flatlands also are the home of four finch species. The large ground finch of Tower is distinctive for having the heaviest bill of any of its species (the same species can show marked differences in some cases, depending on which island or islands it inhabits). The other finches are the sharp-beaked ground finch, the large cactus finch, and the warbler finch.

Among these birds can be found the Galapagos dove and the Tower race of the Galapagos mockingbird, the smallest race of this particular species. There may be nesting great frigate birds established in the tops of the shrubs and small trees, as well, depending on the season. A few of the magnificent frigates nest on the island, too.

After you pass through the scrub brush, the trail comes out to the edge of a large lava field that stretches out before you to the sea. At first it will look as if there is nothing to see, but then you will notice a small creature fluttering low over the lava, and then another. Suddenly you realize that you're seeing the constant movement of hundreds and even thousands of tiny storm petrels circling and twisting in flight. You may see thousands more offshore, like clouds of avian mosquitoes.

Both the wedge-rumped storm petrel (Galapagos storm petrel, *Oceanodroma tethys*) and the band-rumped storm petrel (Madeiran storm petrel, *Oceanodroma castro*) nest in crannies and tunnels beneath the rugged lava field surface.

From the low crest of ground where you stand to see the lava field there are deep and narrow cracks in the earth that harbor one of the major predators of the petrel, particularly the young ones: the short-eared owl *(Asio flammeus)*. It hunts day or night, but when I saw one it was just sitting quietly at the lip of one of the cracks, just a few meters away.

Finally, from your crest vantage point, the view of birds flying along the cliffs can be very rewarding. Red-billed tropicbirds, blue-footed boobies flying in platoons, Galapagos shearwaters *(Puffinus subalaris),* and noddy terns *(Anous stolidus)* all can be seen, complemented by frigates and perhaps red-footed and Nazca boobies returning from far-away fishing sorties.

Hood's marine iguana

5

San Cristobal and Nearby Sites

S an Cristobal is becoming a major tourism site now that its airport is being used as the arrival point for many visitors. The port, Puerto Baquerizo Moreno, is the administrative center for the islands. A ramble down the main street can be enjoyable, and a cool drink often is welcome. Birding in the hills behind the town can be rewarding, too. Your group is likely to be taken to several visitor sites in the higher elevations.

Directly south of San Cristobal is Hood Island. It is the nesting site of the waved albatross, and there are colonies of Nazca and blue-footed boobies. When you land on Hood you are greeted by some of the largest and most colorful of the marine iguanas and usually by lots of sea lions.

West of Hood is Floreana, where there's a good chance to see flamingos and migrating shorebirds in its large, brackish lagoon. For human history, Post Office Bay is the place to go. It's a place that reminds you that Darwin came to this spot, and you'll see mementos of many more recent visitors.

For snorkelers, one of the best moments of the trip can be a quick visit to Devil's Crown, just a few hundred meters off Floreana. This ominous-looking, partially submerged lava cone provides a protected area for swimming. If the weather is good and the sea calm, you'll want to get into your *panga* for the short trip to the middle of the Crown and slip over the side for a few minutes of underwater beauty.

SAN CRISTOBAL (CHATHAM)

San Cristobal, in the far southeast of the archipelago, has had a long, not always pleasant human history. It had no regular inhabitants when Darwin visited for 5 weeks in September 1835. His first view of it (not at the comfortable harbor where you will disembark) was intimidating:

Nothing could be less inviting than the first appearance. A broken field of black, basaltic lava, thrown into the most rugged waves, and crossed by great fissures, is everywhere covered by stunted, sunburnt brushwood, which shows little signs of life. The dry and parched surface, being heated by the

*noonday sun, gave to the air a close and sultry feeling, like that from a stove;
we fancied even that the bushes smelt unpleasantly.* (Darwin, pp. 374–375)

What saved this particular excursion for Darwin was meeting two of the tortoises, something today's visitors are very unlikely to experience because of the very small numbers on this island. He reported,

*The day was glowing hot, and the scramble over the rough surface and through
the intricate thickets, was very fatiguing; but I was well repaid by the strange
Cyclopean scene. As I was walking along I met two large tortoises, each of
which must have weighed two hundred pounds: one was eating a piece of
cactus, and as I approached, it stared at me and slowly stalked away; the
other gave a deep hiss, and drew in its head. These huge reptiles, surrounded
by the black lava, the leafless shrubs, and large cacti, seemed to my fancy like
some antediluvian animals.* (Darwin, pp. 375–376)

In 1841 a small settlement was established on San Cristobal by a group of convicts who rebelled from their brutal treatment in the colony on Floreana. The sagas of the exploitation of convicts or laborers, and of repeated attempts to set up some form of island haven, continued into the twentieth century.

But now San Cristobal is the home of about 8–10,000 people, including farmers and fishing people. It also is the Ecuadorian administrative headquarters for all of the islands. There is a small naval base there and one of the three airstrips in the islands.

Puerto Baquerizo Moreno

Visitors can stroll around the town of Puerto Baquerizo Moreno, pass by the statue of Darwin, go into a local cafe for a cool drink, and check out the small museum and the shops there. Your guide might arrange for the group to take a bus to the highlands.

Now that San Cristobal has an airport and a number of tours start and end there, the town is undergoing some rapid enhancement in its tourist-related facilities. Puerto Baquerizo Moreno also is the jumping-off point for several small excursions to nearby islands. Isla Lobos offers a dry landing, sea lions, and frigate birds. And Kicker Rock and Isla Lobos are impressive sites, often visited on the last afternoon before the departure from the airport at the village. Kicker Rock is a boat-based tour around these dramatic monoliths jutting out of the water. Isla Lobos is a brief land visit.

The Interpretation Center on San Cristobal

This center is a spectacular addition to the islands. It was inaugurated in August 1998. Its supporters included the Spanish government and the government of Ecua-

View of integrated architecture of the Puerto Baquerizo Moreno Interpretation Center

dor. The center is on the edge of Puerto Baquerizo Moreno, and it is reached by a short bus ride, arranged for you by your guide. The center is wonderfully designed to tell the natural and human history of the islands and to serve as an active educational resource for visitors, island schoolchildren, and other residents. It is a beautiful, light, airy building, made of the local stone and wood to blend into the slightly hilly landscape on which it is located. You move easily from room to room, from era to era of archipelago history. The displays are stunning, with luminous portrayals of the geological evolution of the islands and colorful displays of land and marine life.

The human history is told through a combination of paintings, old photographs, and three-dimensional re-creations of early life on the islands. The horrendous story of the penal colony that existed for more than 150 years, until it was closed in 1954 when the appalling conditions there became known internationally, is riveting and dismaying at the same time. The intriguing story of some of the twentieth century's distinctive immigrants from Europe, with broken dreams, divided loyalties, and suspected murders, is equally well told.

For a little break from the learning, take a few minutes to walk outside the building along the boardwalks that extend from it into the surrounding thickets of Palo Santo and other dry, lowland vegetation. The wind sweeps up the hillside from the harbor, and you will have excellent views of the water a kilometer or so away.

El Junco Lagoon

This whole round trip is an easy one and takes only 2 to 3 hours, depending on how much time the group takes enjoying the birding and the view. This small freshwater lake is located at about 700 meters elevation. It is one of the few lakes in the islands that does not go dry periodically. The lake and its shores are an excellent place for birding, and the trip up to it takes you through several vegetation zones. You reach the lake by bus, a trip that is arranged by your captain or guide, and you will pass into the more humid levels of the island, where farming takes place.

The view of the lake itself is lovely, and the birding is a wonderful mixture of shorebirds, drawn by the fresh water, and the island's distinctive land birds. The lake attracts whimbrels, stilts, white-cheeked pintail ducks, and common gallinules.

As for land birds, seven of the Darwin's finches are listed as being here. Telling one from another is a challenge. You might be particularly lucky and see a warbler finch here, with its tiny thin bill. It's hard to believe it is actually a finch.

FLOREANA (SANTA MARIA, CHARLES)

Floreana is located at the southern edge of the archipelago and almost exactly at the center of its east–west dimension. It is about a 3- to 5-hour trip from the south coast of Santa Cruz or from Española (Hood) to its east.

Several families still live on this island, about 100 people in all. There is even a tiny tea shop there at Black Beach. Relatives of one of the Europeans who settled

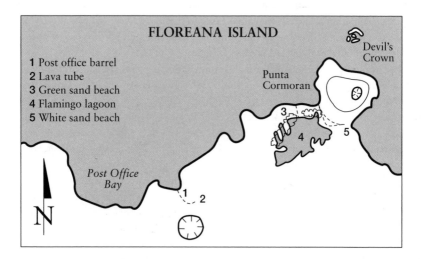

FLOREANA ISLAND

1 Post office barrel
2 Lava tube
3 Green sand beach
4 Flamingo lagoon
5 White sand beach

Devil's Crown
Punta Cormoran

Post Office Bay

N

here in the 1930s operate the shop. On my last visit we stopped for cold drinks but found the prices of mementos to be higher than those in Puerto Ayora or Puerto Baquerizo Moreno.

There are four visitor land sites on Floreana: Punta Cormoran, with its flamingo lagoon and its two lovely beaches; Post Office Bay, still the place to send mail to friends around the world; a lava tube that can be followed far underground; and Asilo de la Paz, the site in the highlands where pirates once came for water.

Just northwest of Punta Cormoran is Devil's Crown, an excellent diving site, usually reached from the Punta Cormoran anchorage.

Punta Cormoran

Punta Cormoran is a steep, small lava cone on a point of land joined to the larger island by a low-lying strip of vegetated dune. You approach the site by a wet landing in a pleasant cove. The beach sand itself is of interest because it has a large proportion of olivine crystals, derived from volcanic action, which have a pale olive color.

You move up the usual beach slope, passing through the dune vegetation. Shortly, the trail ascends slightly along a hill that faces the Punta cone itself. At the high point of the trail, only a few minutes from the start, you look down into a large lagoon. Its water level varies greatly, from mostly mud flats to nearly a lake (in an El Niño year). At any time, it is likely to be an excellent place for birdwatching. Flamingos are common. From this height you can see the underwater trails they make through the mud as they sieve through the turbid water to extract minute crustaceans. At first you may think the lines are the traces of cracks that were formed in the mud when it was very dry, but then as you follow a flamingo's movements you see that these curving, wobbling lines are made by their feet shuffling through the mud.

The edges of the lagoon, particularly on the northwest side, have vegetation right to the water and are good for spotting shorebirds. We saw a phalarope (no one could decide which species), a willet, and white-cheeked pintail ducks. Whimbrels, semi-palmated plovers, and wandering tattlers are regularly seen there in small numbers, too.

Don't forget to look at the birdlife right around you at the viewpoint. I had an excellent look at the Galapagos large-billed flycatcher, complete with an insect gripped in its beak. There are a variety of the finches, with small and medium ground finches and the cactus finch listed as abundant in the bird guide.

After your pause at the viewpoint, you will go about 350 meters farther to one of the best beaches in the islands. It lines a shallow cove with the finest white sand. It is like granulated sugar, and populating the sand are multitudes of ghost crabs. They hide from your approach and then come up from their tiny holes to skitter down the beach in search of food. You'll be lucky to see them because of their shyness and the difficulty of picking out their pale, translucent bodies, even when they are above ground.

Once when we were at this beach, it was visited by a number of rays, probably stingrays, which were about a meter across. They came right up to the water's edge, just skimming along well within view.

We swam here once, in the El Niño year, when the water was about 77°F (25°C), and it remains one of our best memories. The ground falls away gradually, and there were no waves or currents. It was like our own private pool, just right for gently stroking from one side of the cove to the other or for standing quietly in the water and watching the light change on the Palo Santo that clothe Floreana's graceful slopes.

Post Office Bay

Post Office Bay is just a short boat ride to the west of Punta Cormoran. You land on a brown beach, perhaps sharing it with a few sea lions, and walk beyond the beach a couple of minutes to a small clearing in the scrub. This is not a prepossessing place. It looks very tired and worn, with few redeeming features. But you are here for its human history, for that big wooden barrel that still holds mail for the world.

The barrel is covered with signs from boats that have visited over the years. People seem to have made the signs themselves, raiding wooden slats from driftwood or even using plaques that have their boat name carved in them. It is interesting to see the variety of names and places from which they came. And it's completely contained, right on the barrel and its little pedestal, so it's the only acceptable graffiti in the islands. Visitors love to send mail via this method. Guides will open the little door and pull out a handful of envelopes. They check for letters that other visitors want sent. If one goes to your country, then you take it along, stamp it when you get there, and mail it. You might even attach a note telling the addressee when you picked it up. We sent some off as soon as we got to our home airport, and the ones that we had deposited in the barrel were delivered before we got home ourselves, so it's pretty effective.

The Lava Tube

This lava tube is harder to enter than the ones in the highlands of Santa Cruz. It starts out as a hole in the flat ground about 10 minutes' walk past the post office barrel. A wooden staircase descends 5 meters or so to the first level spot.

There's a low-ceilinged shaft down to the floor. You will walk a few minutes along the smooth bottom until you encounter water. Visitors then tend to take off their shoes and continue through the deepening water, walking and even half-swimming to reach the end of the cave. I haven't been into these tubes, but my teenage nephews have and they told me that they enjoyed it.

This whole excursion to the tube end and back takes about an hour.

Asilo de la Paz

This is a very historic and beautiful area in the highlands of Floreana. The Asilo de la Paz is the place where drinking water has always been available. Somehow the pirates discovered this fact hundreds of years ago; how they did so, considering that the location is 5 miles from the little harbor of Puerto Valasco Ibarra, is amazing, but somehow it happened.

You will get there on a bus arranged by your guide. The drive up from the harbor takes about an hour. You can distinguish the different vegetation zones as you go along. However, they are not very precise in general, and because some of the area is not within the park and there is farming and ranching, there is quite a mix of vegetation types as you go along. You'll also see some of the homes of

Medium tree finch on Floreana

View from the Floreana Highlands across the valley and up to an extinct volcanic cone

people who live on the island, with children waving at you as you go by.

The Asilo site is not within park boundaries. It is part of the agricultural zone of the islands. However, the Park has established a very large "corral" for some 30 tortoises that were once kept by locals as pets. Here you can wander at leisure and get close to the tortoises for photographs. As you approach the Asilo site, you will notice the coolness and humidity of the higher elevations. The guide will take you past a residence up to a moist, fern- and moss-studded cliff face. It has a shallow horizontal indentation, about the size of a *panga*, and water seeps through the striations and cracks of that concave part of the cliff face—a steady but very small drip of water. It can't be called a stream of water because it is not. There are about four drips, one of which was being collected by a local resident for personal use with the help of a 3-liter plastic jug, turned upside down with the bottom cut open to make a wider mouth for receiving the precious fluid. This container had its own hose leading down the hillside. The rest of the water is collected in a tub, and it makes its way along whatever piping system there is for the remainder of the residents. It must take at least 30 minutes to collect 1 gallon. It is almost incomprehensible that a whole human history, from pirates to adventurous European settlers and now their descendants and other locals, was made possible by that tiny, tedious supply of water.

The other artifacts you will see on this visit are the pirate caves. These are the smallest caves for human habitation that one could imagine. They are little more than two or three vertical indentations in a few cliff faces, and they may have been hollowed out further by hand. Surely no more than two or three hardy, begrimed souls at any one time could have found shelter here. There are still the smudges of fires from yesteryear, but still it is hard to fathom that anyone could make this even a temporary home. The whole place makes you keenly aware of water as a life-giving, life-saving element.

After your visit to the water source and the pirate caves, you probably will go on a little tour of the more open land surrounding the area. The birding there is excellent, and it is one of your chances to see the medium tree finch. We saw it in a plantation area and even photographed it. The guides were extremely pleased to have made this identification. For me, even as I snapped the picture, the finches had long since become almost indistinguishable. That tends to happen toward the end of a trip.

The wide-open view overlooking the slopes down from the highlands and out to the sea is one of the best in the islands.

Devil's Crown

Devil's Crown, also called Onslow Island, is a small but very exciting place to visit. It is located just 250 meters from Floreana's shore, a few minutes' *panga* ride from the Punta Cormoran anchorage. If no one is snorkeling or scuba diving, the boat probably will circle the Crown a couple of times so you can get a good view from the medium distance. Devil's Crown is the partially exposed cone of an extinct volcano. Its once-complete circle of rock has been broken in several places, allowing the sea to come in. Its black sides are so steep, craggy, and harsh-looking that it's easy to see how it could acquire this sinister name.

The walls are splashed at the top with the whitewash of bird excrement, and the only thing that seems to grow there are two kinds of cactus (*Jasminocereus thouarsii*, the candelabra cactus, and *Opuntia megasperma*, the prickly pear). But birds love the place, and you can see red-billed tropicbirds, pelicans, lava gulls, and frigate birds sitting on the jagged rocks, loafing or waiting for the right time to go out to feed. Even the occasional heron can be seen there.

If you get a chance to go snorkeling or scuba diving in the center of the Crown, you will be very glad you did. Your mother-boat will send you over in very small groups to the site itself. The *panga* will be tethered to a line that is attached to a big concrete block at the western side of the inner circle. (This is to prevent descending anchors from destroying the rich life that clings to the rocks and strews the ocean floor.)

Although the currents outside the Crown can be fierce, and the surrounding sea

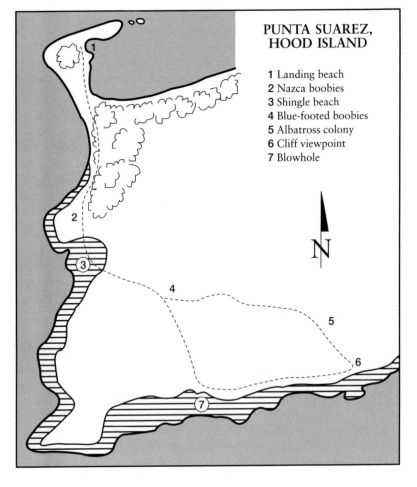

PUNTA SUAREZ,
HOOD ISLAND

1 Landing beach
2 Nazca boobies
3 Shingle beach
4 Blue-footed boobies
5 Albatross colony
6 Cliff viewpoint
7 Blowhole

N

is known as a good place for shark-watching, the inside is a more welcoming place. You will always be near your *panga*, and you can rest awhile on the tiny beach that is exposed at low tide. And the underwater life is dreamlike in its beauty and variety. From huge sea lions whipping past you to layer upon layer of different fish species to the sea stars, tube corals, and sea cucumbers on the bottom, there is enough to occupy you for hours. (My favorites were the schools of needlefish that hung by the hundreds right at the top of the water, gleaming in the light from above.) The cold of the water probably will force you out long before your interest has waned. Divers will want to use full wet-dry suits.

Even if you aren't much of a swimmer and hate cold water, do try to snorkel here (assuming it is a calm enough day that the captain feels it would be safe for all). I found myself uneasy here on my one snorkeling adventure because of the cold water, so I held onto the captain's hand and we paddled lazily along, he the courteous gentleman as always. Just ask for a buddy and you'll have one instantly.

Española (Hood)

Española/Hood is a fairly flat island, rising slightly from sea level on its north side to rugged black cliffs perhaps 30 meters high on its south side. The landing there is one of the more exciting you will have because the boat has to anchor about 200 meters or more out to sea. Depending on the tides, the *panga* must take a circuitous route over barely submerged rocks, through real ocean waves, to get to the sheltered calm of its landing place. Extra caution with the cameras is called for here; keep them well protected.

Once you land you are immediately in the midst of such numbers and variety of wildlife that it is almost too much to absorb. First you will be greeted by the endemic Española/ Hood mockingbird. There are likely to be many sea lions, both in the little cove and right on shore where you disembark. Then within a few steps you see dozens, even hundreds of marine iguanas on the rocks at the back edge of the sandy beach.

These iguanas are not like any others in the islands. They are the same *species,* but the Hood *race* is very distinct for having the largest average size of all marine iguanas and for its striking coloring. It has patches of dark red on its sides, a greenish tinge along its ridged back, and the usual black everywhere else.

If you see lava lizards, these are a species unique to Española *(Microlophus delanonis).* These are the largest lava lizards in the islands; they are also notable for having the shortest, thickest tail. The female has red under her chin and at the base of her tail. The male is speckled black, yellow, and green.

Within just a few more steps you will reach the first approach to a cliff edge, where you will see a nesting area for Nazca boobies. They have a yearly breeding cycle, starting in November with egg laying and ending in June when the young are able to fly and feed on their own. Next you will descend for a few meters to a small shingle beach and then go back up to the open expanses of low scrub and open areas that cover the island.

Your next treat is a large nesting area for blue-footed boobies. They do not have the distinctively defined breeding season of the Nazca boobies, and you may see eggs or any stage of development in the young at any time of year.

Beautiful Galapagos doves will be pecking and probing on the ground here and there. They seem less wary of people here than they do on other islands. Completely unwary and actually very aggressive is the Hood mockingbird *(Mimus macdonaldi),* which is found only here and on a nearby rocky islet, Gardner-near-Hood. It is somewhat larger than the other three mockingbird species found on the islands, and it has a heavier, more downcurved beak. It has hazel-colored eyes. You will get close enough to see the color of those eyes because these mockers are nearly pestiferous in their approach to people. They hop on your shoes, sit on your hat, and jump on your packsack. You can get the most "touristy" pictures without trying to lure them to you. They come whether you like it or not.

Scan the bushes for the large-billed race of the large cactus finch *(Geospiza conirostris)* and a very gray warbler finch subspecies *(Certhidea olivacea)*. The small ground finch *(Geospiza fuliginosa)* nests on the island, and so does the large-billed flycatcher.

Then, only about 400 meters from the beginning of the trail, you will come to the only place where the waved albatross nests (with the exception of a few pairs that nest on a tiny island off the coast of Ecuador). The 12,000 pairs that nest yearly on Hood are, effectively, the entire population of this bird in the world. For the nature lover there is something moving about being within a few meters of all the varied activity that goes on as these birds lay their eggs and care for their young.

The setting is quite dramatic, for you are near the edge of high, black cliffs, with the waves far below rolling in from the open sea to the east. Many kinds of seabirds sit next to you on the rocks, and others soar above and below you. And every few minutes, especially in the early morning, a huge albatross waddles to the edge of the cliff, makes a few awkward wing flaps, and then launches itself out on the updrafts to become one of the world's most graceful and efficient soaring beings.

Depending on when you are there, you may see a great deal of the elaborate display these birds make as they claim and maintain territory or as they form their pairs and trade off the care of their young at the nest. They mate for life, so only birds mating for their first time, at 4 or 5 years of age, will be doing the pair-formation or courtship displays to any great degree. However, toward the end of the breeding season, already established pairs will do displays like this as they consolidate their relationship for the year to come.

There are several detailed descriptions of the displays in the scientific literature, but to the uninitiated, the central theme of the courtship movement seems to be variations on fencing. The birds cross bills, click them, throw their heads high, make loud honking noises, and then resume the thrust and dodge of their bills. It's noisy and exciting to watch. Part of the display is a vast exaggeration of their ordinary rolling walk, a gait that makes them look like the most drunken and macho sailor just hitting dry land after months in a very small boat at sea.

The breeding season of this albatross is from the end of March through December, with August to December being the most active times. To see the huge eggs, the adorably ugly chicks, and the waddling adults that turn into incomparably fine flyers is to participate in one of the premier privileges of visiting the Galapagos.

On your way back from the albatross grounds the trail traces the cliff edges and you will have an excellent view of the blowhole that shoots a plume of spray 15 to

30 meters in the air. There is a crevice at sea level where the surging water rushes in and is then almost trapped except for this one upward exit. The spume is impressive to watch, but visitors are no longer allowed to descend the cliff and experience the spray close up.

Keep your binoculars ready for viewing along the shoreline because the area is a good one for seeing shorebirds such as the oystercatcher, a few of which breed on Hood. The rocky cliffs are nesting places for the swallow-tailed gull, the red-billed tropicbird, and Audubon's shearwater.

Penquin seen from boat

6

Isabela and Nearby Sites

Isabela and Fernandina seem more rugged and inaccessible than the other islands of the Galapagos, partly because a number of the visitor sites are many hours by boat from the central core of Santa Cruz and Santiago. Not all itineraries can include visits to the west side of Isabela because of the limitations brought on by time, weather, sea conditions and distance. Trips to Urbina Bay to see its recently uplifted coral beds or to Punta Espinoza on Fernandina involve long and tiring trips on seas that are rarely calm. In any case, you will often see Isabela's Volcan Alcedo or other looming volcanoes as your trip takes you between the island and Santiago or Santa Cruz.

ISABELA (ALBEMARLE)

Isabela is the largest of all the islands of the Galapagos. It is on the west side of the archipelago. It is very narrow but more than 100 kilometers long, running directly north to south. Its most narrow point, the Perry Isthmus, is about one third up from the southern edge of the island.

Isabela has the most imposing terrain in the islands, composed as it is of six towering shield volcanoes that have merged over the millennia, forming the mountainous profile seen today. Two of the six volcanoes (Wolf and Cerro Azul) are more than 1700 meters high. Alcedo, located at the north–south midpoint of the island, is about 1200 meters high.

Because Isabela is far from the central islands of the archipelago and because the trip to its far side is very time-consuming and can be very rough, most visitors will be fortunate to be able to visit one or two sites at most. They are fascinating, and one, Urbina Bay, is quite exotic, even for the Galapagos.

Tagus Cove

Tagus Cove is a seldom-visited site on the northwest side of Isabela. There are two activities for the visitor, one on land and the other on water. The land trip is a short walk up to Darwin Lake, which is a saltwater lagoon that is actually above sea level. The slopes are clothed with typical arid zone vegetation. The chief draws of the visit are a good selection of birds, getting a good view of a crater lake, and views of Darwin and Wolf volcanoes.

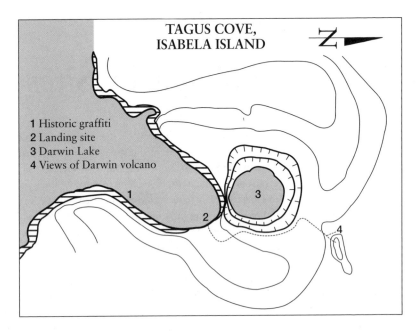

Upon landing, you may find a couple of flightless cormorant nests. When on the trail, there will probably be a variety of finches, possibly even the woodpecker finch. There may be mockingbirds and even evidence of tortoises, if not the beasts themselves. This also is often a great area for seeing the Galapagos hawk.

The cliffs that enfold the bay are marred by extensive graffiti, put there by crews and passengers of many of the ships that have come here over the years. The ones that are very old have some historical interest, but fortunately this practice has been sufficiently discouraged that it has become almost extinct.

The other activity for visitors is a ride in the *panga* along the cliffs. There are shelves of rock near the entrance of the cove and here you may see a few Galapagos penguins and flightless cormorants. Blue-footed boobies are common, and there may be marine iguanas. The *panga* ride is a very pleasant way to see the sea-based wildlife from another perspective, although it can be difficult to photograph from the gently rocking boat.

Urbina Bay

Urbina Bay is also on the west coast of Isabela, directly west of Volcan Alcedo. There is a wet landing, and if the seas are high, you may not be able to land—the beach is steep and surf can be heavy. Once on land, however, you come to what looks like just another scrubby plain stretching out beyond. But this area is extremely interesting because it has a dramatic and beautiful example of the geological activity of the islands: In 1954, 5 kilometers of the marine reef at the edge of the shore were uplifted 4 meters.

No one was there at the time, but not too long afterward a Disney film crew was sailing in the area and they noticed that the beach area gleamed unusually white. As they got closer, they saw that this whiteness was caused by conglomerates of coral and calcium-based algae that were out of their watery element. On these uplifted rocks were stranded sea animals—lobsters, marine turtles, and even fish—in the pools in the pitted surface. Obviously, if these active animals had been trapped like that, the whole event must have happened very quickly.

Exactly why it happened is not clear, but the likelihood is that some subterranean shift of molten lava, perhaps caused by volcanic activity on Alcedo or the more southern Sierra Negra volcano, was responsible for this movement of the earth's crust.

For today's visitor, it can be a very odd sensation to walk on dry land right in the

Tagus Cove slopes, luxuriantly green in an El Niño year

middle of a bed of coral, with large boulders of it almost waist-high. (The globular coral, curiously brainlike in surface texture, is now dull black.) It is also a beautiful place, with the clumps of coral with their intricate surfaces, and the remnants of barnacles, sea shells, sea worms, and other creatures embedded in them or strewn about on the ground.

FERNANDINA (NARBOROUGH)

Fernandina, the farthest west of the Galapagos Islands, is one of the most volcanically active in the archipelago. Because of its distance from the center of the islands and because it is a particularly lengthy trip to reach it, this island is visited rarely by touring groups. It is an intriguing place and well worth the trip if it can be managed.

Fernandina is about 1500 meters high, with its main crater about 6.5 kilometers wide. It is one of the newest islands. It does not have the rich floral life that some of the other islands of its height display, partly because so much of it has been coated with recent lava flows and volcanic ash and partly because Isabela's heights capture much of the rain it might get from moist air coming from the east.

Fernandina's volcano has erupted several times in the twentieth century. In 1968 it erupted and the floor of its crater, already 610 meters below its rim, dropped another few hundred meters. In 1977 the volcano erupted again, sending rivers of lava into its lake from a crack in the crater wall. The next year another eruption occurred, with more lava spewed into the crater. The most spectacular eruption was in January 1995. It erupted again in May, 2000. But unless you are here at one of those special explosive times, you will be seeing only the outside slopes of this crater, along with sweeps of black lava from flows that happened before our time.

Punta Espinoza

The landing site itself is on a spit of black lava rock, reminiscent of the recent flows of Sullivan Bay. The landing is a dry one in a tiny, mangrove-lined inlet. Sometimes there are many marine iguanas right at the landing site, on the rocks. The trail goes in two directions, to the left to a field of harsh, sharp "a-a" lava and to the right to the "land's end." I was able to visit only the area to the right.

The point itself has rich and varied wildlife, even if the surroundings are stark and barren, except for the small patches of mangrove where you land. In ordinary times there are nesting flightless cormorants and penguins, and a number of marine iguanas perched on the rocks and on bits of driftwood stuck in the cracks in the lava.

I was there in an El Niño year, and there was an ominous quality to the whole point. There was but one flightless cormorant to be seen and the distressing sight of a lone sea lion pup, its ribs showing through its fur, leaning against a piece of

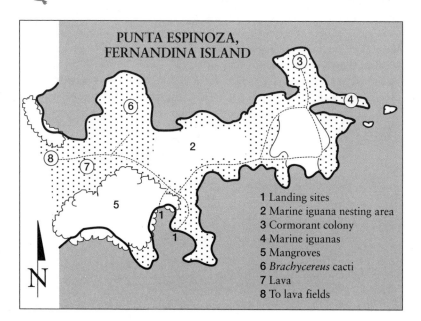

PUNTA ESPINOZA,
FERNANDINA ISLAND

1 Landing sites
2 Marine iguana nesting area
3 Cormorant colony
4 Marine iguanas
5 Mangroves
6 *Brachycereus* cacti
7 Lava
8 To lava fields

driftwood, seemingly with not long to live. (Few young ones did survive that year.) It was late in the afternoon, and we'd had an exhausting voyage to this place. It all seemed a dull monochrome: gray sky, black rocks, gray spines of driftwood, dark iguanas, dully colored sea lion pup. We all felt very gray ourselves and hoped to come back the next day to spend more time and exorcise our depression, but heavy seas prevented it.

Your own visit undoubtedly will have its own character, most likely an exciting and illuminating one. If you have a chance to examine the mangrove area, there

Fernandina's lagoons are great for birdwatching

should be a variety of herons. Yellow warblers and mockingbirds are found here, too. The great blue herons and some pelicans nest here. The birding guide says that the Galapagos rail and mangrove finch have been reported here in the past, but not recently. The shore area is a good place to look for migrant shorebirds and for petrels, shearwaters, and frigate birds. The Galapagos shearwaters apparently fly inland at night to roost in the crevices of the broken lava fields. The frigate birds sleep in the mangroves.

Small-motor sailer at anchor near Sante Fe Island

Part III
TRAVEL TIPS

1

Are the Islands for You?

The Galapagos Islands are a very special place, but they are not suitable for every traveler. Part II of this book has taken you to most of the sites where you are likely to go. That will have told you some things about the pleasures and rigors of such a trip, but the following material is written specifically to help you decide whether you are a likely candidate for this adventure, considering the kind and amount of travel involved, the living conditions, approximate cost of a trip, and the physical and mental requirements. At the end of this section is a brief discussion of travel in mainland Ecuador. For those who are getting ready to go, there is a list of things to bring with you and a section of tips for photography in these demanding conditions. Finally, Appendix C provides information on how you can support the ongoing work of those dedicated to restoring and preserving these beloved islands.

Typical harbor inhabitants taking it easy

2
Planning a Visit

The Galapagos wildlife is very free, but the visitors are a highly controlled element of the environment. You can visit the park segments only in a registered and licensed boat and only with a trained licensed guide. The boats are available almost exclusively through travel agents and tour operators who subcontract to Ecuadorian tourism operators for the services described in their brochures and trip plans. You can deal directly with Ecuadorian tour operators through the Internet or you can travel via a tour company in your home country.

MAKING ARRANGEMENTS

Although you should go through a travel agent or tour operator, you have some real choices with either kind of arrangement. It is entirely possible to book your

The Puerto Baquerizo Moreno Airport reception area is built from local materials.

own flights, through a travel agent or on your own with an airline, to Quito and the islands. You can minimize costs by booking your own flights and having your travel agent book hotels in Quito or Miami (the usual jumping-off place), but this can mean a little more uncertainty if your hotel in Ecuador has lost your booking or you are not comfortable taking taxis out of airports where they do not speak a lot of English. I've done it both ways and there are advantages and glitches with each. The actual boat time must be booked through an agent. If you go as part of any group, perhaps with a birding club or your local natural history museum, it is likely that this tour will include all the bookings of flights and accommodation on the way as well as the boat time in the islands.

As of 2005, the principal airlines that originate in the United States and fly to Quito are American Airlines and Continental. There is also TAME, the Ecuadorian government airline. The main gateways from the United States to Quito are Miami and Houston.

It is best to book the three-stage flight all at once (your home, Quito, Galapagos, and return) if you are doing it yourself because the round-trip flight from Quito to the islands alone, if booked separately, is $450 U.S. but would be appreciably less when a part of a three-stage flight package. When you are pricing tours, it might be a good idea to compare these costs and the average costs per night on the various boats to see whether you think a particular arrangement is acceptably priced for you. Also, visitors from the United Kingdom probably can keep their costs down by booking low-cost flights to Canada and then carrying on their trip from there.

There is a very wide range of prices and types of boats to choose from through standard traveling channels. Do one or all of the following: check the Internet for background on the islands and for listings of many tour operators, see your travel agent, call the Ecuadorian consul nearest you, check your favorite nature magazine for tour company advertisements, and talk with friends. You probably won't have to go far to find someone who has made the trip or at least knows someone who has.

Because the Internet is revolutionizing travel planning, be sure to use it as you prepare for your trip. Here are a couple of useful websites to get you started.

For background information on Galapagos National Park, you'll need to do a Web search. For information on the Charles Darwin Research Station and Foundation, the website is *www.darwinfoundation.org.*

An excellent site for locating tour operators who have joined together to help maintain the best standards of tourism to the islands is *www.igtoa.org,* the home page of the International Galapagos Tour Operators Association (IGTOA). This consortium of tour operators that specialize in travel to the Galapagos is united in a common goal: "To preserve the Galapagos Islands as a unique world heritage that can provide education, adventure, and inspiration for future generations of travelers." The IGTOA website is www.igtoa.org/info_for_travelers/

PLANNING THE LENGTH OF A VISIT

First, the trip to the islands is a long one from almost anywhere, even for Ecuadorians who fly or sail the 1000 kilometers from the mainland to get there. From just about anywhere in the United States or Canada, you should expect a full day's travel to reach Quito. When scheduling your trip, it is essential that you allow yourself at least 24 hours in Quito before the planned departure for the islands themselves. This trip in itself can be very tiring; also, Quito is more than 3000 meters in altitude, so it is common for people to suffer somewhat from the thin air. (Just take it easy, don't rush about, drink lots of water, and rest often.) You may want to consult your physician before leaving about the use of diuretics to reduce headaches, but that is a decision for the two of you. I found it helpful on my latest trip, but you may not find it necessary or appropriate.

The conditions in Quito are relevant to travelers; I strongly recommend that visitors spend at least two weeks in mainland Ecuador, interspersing a day or two in Quito, then taking a small-scale "package" tour for a few days in the Highlands, stopping over in various towns and villages and staying in the beautiful haciendas and lodges that abound. I did this with a few of us and an excellent guide/interpreter, in a sparkling clean van, and we had a marvelous time. Also, you really must spend four or five days in one of the lodges in the Amazon rain forest, toward the eastern edges of Ecuador.

It is possible to visit the Galapagos for as little as 3 nights. Although it may seem that you can save money by shortening your cruise, this option is my least favored one for two reasons. First, you're spending the same amount of money to fly to the Galapagos Islands whether you choose a standard 7-night cruise or a shorter 3- or 4-night cruise. The per diem cost of a cruise also doesn't drop significantly because of a shorter trip, and you will see less of the islands. Second, short cruises usually are offered by large cruise boats that carry about 90 passengers. In this mode of travel you can visit only a limited range of sites, because the large number of visitors can cause too much wear and tear on a place, so the more fragile ones are visited by the smaller, less "populated" boats. If you are on one of the biggest boats, visitors are broken up into groups of 16 each for visiting any given site. This is the maximum allowed per guide while on land and it can be a crowded situation. You will want to decide if you would rather have the smaller scaled and perhaps more personalized experience that is more likely when traveling in one of the smaller boats. On the other hand, if your time is limited and you like the idea of being on a substantial luxury cruise ship, taking a day and a half each for the trip to and from Guayaquil, then this could be the choice for you.

The standard trip stay for mid-size to smaller boats is 8 days, 7 nights, although you can also book trips for about two weeks. More than 80 ships currently operate cruises in the Galapagos. The carrying capacity of passengers ranges from 6 to a maximum of 100 on the largest boats.

The boats come in a range of sizes, comfort levels, and prices. (Always remember that the same boat may have one price for one tour group or travel agent and

Checking the sails

another price for a different one. This all depends on the business practices of the agent or tour operator, so do compare.) The smaller boats carry 6 to 20 people. A few of them are motor–sailers, which adds another element of adventure to the trip (and a calmer ride with the sails up).

The Park prefers that tours last no longer than eight days, and I think that for most people that is really a reasonable time for a visit, especially if it is in one of the smaller boats (and the larger ones don't have longer trips anyway.) The reasoning for this is based on a combination of factors such as costs, completeness of island coverage, and overall ambiance of a trip taken in the small-boat conditions.

However, it must be emphasized that travel to the islands is generally geared to the 8-day, 7-night trip, and this strategy works very well indeed. If you have young children along, 8 days probably is the comfort limit for all concerned.

TIME OF YEAR FOR VISITING

You will find a great deal to see at most times of the year in the Galapagos. However, there are a few general guidelines to keep in mind. The high seasons for visitation are December to March and July and August. So book early for these times. In the autumn many of the boats are in dry dock and the guides are on refresher courses, so there will be fewer boats to choose from at that time.

As for weather, the mildest and driest times generally are October to early December and May to August; March tends to be the worst month for inclement weather. Seas are calmer, and days are bright without being unbearably hot on land (on the water, in the moving boat, heat is rarely a problem). Water temperatures are much cooler from June to September (about 18°C). Think about bringing a wetsuit for snorkeling at these times if you want to do more than leap in and out for a quick glimpse below the surface. (Of course, if you are scuba diving you will want a full wet–dry suit for your comfort and safety.)

Rain is not often a disruptive factor unless you are in the midst of an El Niño event, when rain can be very heavy at times. The El Niño current sweeps down to the islands on an irregular basis, so it is almost impossible to plan around it. Just book for when you want to go and take your chances. I've been there during one of these events and it had its own fascination.

3
Trip Cost and Living Conditions on the Boat

Nearly all travel agents and tour operators around the world draw on the pool of about 80 boats that are licensed to operate in the islands. The boats I have traveled on and the others I've seen while there are clean, have good guides and cooks, and are a good value for the money at whatever level of cost and service you chose. Things change quickly in the islands, so I won't recommend specific boats. The important thing is to ask around among your friends or see whether your travel agent or tour operator has been to the islands recently and find out which boat he or she were on. Just do your research and read your brochures carefully, and you are very likely to have a wonderful time. Here are some basic questions to ask when planning your trip.

• Does the price of the trip include the Galapagos National Park Fee and Quito–Galapagos airfare? Make sure all additional costs to you are specifically outlined from the outset.

• What kind of naturalist guide is on board? Ask whether he or she is an experienced guide. All naturalists are trained and licensed by the Galapagos National Park Service. Some of them speak as many as three languages fluently, and the person you are likely to have as your guide probably will have at least 2 years of guiding experience. Certainly, if you come from an English-speaking country, your guide will be fluent in English.

• Does the boat include snorkeling equipment, and, if so, is it included in the price of the trip? By the way, kayaking is is only permitted by authorized boats within the park boundaries, although land based kayaking is permitted for local operators near the main towns. Some boats provide wetsuits on board or have them for rental. (Remember, scuba diving is another matter; see comments below.)

The cost and luxury levels of the boats vary widely, from the strictly utilitarian to the very fancy. However, keep in mind that prices for the same boat can vary a lot, according to the pricing structure of the travel agent or tour operator. It depends on the volume of business and business decisions the operator makes.

The price you would pay for the islands segment of your trip ranges from about $300 U.S. per day to as high as $600. But the majority of the boats that offer good

Safety briefing on the first day on the boat

service will be at the middle of this scale.

You'll find a great deal of this information, including photos of many of the boats, maps of the routes, and likely itineraries on the 'net. The itinerary can change on the spot, however, if weather conditions or park policies—say in the case of a fire on the island—call for this. Flexibility is the watchword for captain, crew, and visitors. The International Galapagos Tour Operators' Association one (*www.igtoa.org*) is always a good place to start. Also, your travel agent or tour operator should be able to show you recent pictures of the available boats, including information on navigational equipment, expected itinerary, average speed, drawings of the complete internal layout, notation on number of bunks per room, and number of toilets. This information is essential for your decision making. If your agent or tour operator can't provide this kind of material, *go to a different one.* Shop around for what travel agents can offer and compare with organized group tours, such as natural history societies, which often have their own special emphasis. These specialized tours may have their own group leaders who may be birding or natural history experts. Of course, the boat will have its own locally trained naturalist guide, as they all must have. Your tour company's "leader" should have a collaborative relationship with the naturalist guide, but the guide and captain are the ultimate "authority" for the group.

With all this discussion of prices and cabins and planning, it may sound as if the whole adventure can be predicted or that if you figure out some exact calculation of cost and space you'll know exactly what will happen. However, the Galapagos is one of those travel destinations where the quality of the experience is not predicated largely on cost. This is because the Galapagos visit is not and cannot be a totally predetermined experience. Humans, animals, machines, weather, seasons, and just plain luck all work together to shape your trip. Each boat has its captain, crew, cook, and naturalist guide. A good cook or a good guide can make a trip a totally rewarding experience. The opposite is also true. But the size or cost of the boat does not determine the quality of the cooking, guiding, or of your overall experience.

4
Physical and Mental Requirements

G iven the distance and potential expense of a trip such as this, it is important to have a good match between the person and the destination. The best approximation of the overall rigors of the trip would be a 2-week backpacking trip, only someone else carries your load and cooks the food. Not terribly rough, in other words, but still demanding a degree of patience and energy. The element that must be added to this is that it is ocean camping. That 15- to 90-meter-long boat is your home. Those people are your companions. That ocean is not going to go away. In terms of mental outlook, people who can roll with the punches (and the

Typical wet landing and return

Typical group portrait taken at Post Office Bay on Floreana Island

ocean swells), who like to be with people but still can find amusement in quiet reading or journal writing in the evenings, and who love the outdoors in all its endless variety will be very glad they went.

In physical terms, the person who is basically healthy and can scamper up and down a ladder on the side of a heaving boat, get in and out of a lunging wooden *panga* or motorboat at the shore, walk a couple of hours now and then in blazing sun, and withstand a chilly breeze and the slap of a wave across the face will be very happy on the trip.

I suggest that you be able to swim and generally be comfortable around water. You won't have to swim, but it is an appealing option at times. The main thing is that you not find ocean living distressing in any way. In practical terms, the crew will start out with an orientation to safety measures on board, and you're required to wear a life jacket on the short trips in the little *panga* (rubber or wooden dinghy) that ferries you between the shore and your boat, so that is reassuring.

A WORD ABOUT CHILDREN

Children certainly do make the trip to the Galapagos. Only travel-hardened children at least 7 years old should be taken, in my experience. Older children are more likely to enjoy themselves and not be a trial to others.

First, I strongly suggest that children be good swimmers. They are not more likely to fall overboard than an adult, but they probably will be much more interested in swimming. It can be very appealing for them to be able to look forward to swimming in the slow times, assuming the water is warm enough. Also, it is the adult who will be responsible for them and worrying about them, so parents should do themselves a favor and make sure the child swims well.

Most importantly, children (and adults) must be mature enough to understand that the Galapagos Islands are a natural treasure. That means behavior that might be tolerated elsewhere (such as running off in a different direction, not paying attention to directions from the naturalist guide) cannot be tolerated here and can be dangerous on cliffs and in other hazardous areas. If a child can understand that straying off the marked path may destroy part of a very fragile ecosystem, then certainly he or she should be ready for what may well be the adventure of a lifetime.

It's not all learning—there's time to relax.

If a child has a highly developed sense of curiosity, is fairly patient with long boat rides where there may be "nothing to do" except sit or read or draw, and can put up with sunburn or seasickness and unfamiliar food, then the trip will be fine. For any child under 14 or so, a weeklong trip may be about the limit of physical and psychological tolerance.

5
What to Bring

The following are the essentials that every Galapagos visitor should bring for an 8-day trip. It does not include what you might want to bring for any time you spend in mainland Ecuador. (For that, add one heavier pair of slacks and a polar fleece jacket. Plan to buy one of the wonderful bulky locally made sweaters and caps at a market or on the street. You'll look like a tourist, but you'll be dressed perfectly for the Quito altitude.)

CLOTHING

Make as many of these items hand-washable and easy to dry as possible:
2 pairs long pants, lightweight (zip-off legs are great)
2 or 3 pairs sturdy, lightweight shorts
1 bathing suit
1-week supply underwear
2 or 3 tank tops
2 or 3 short-sleeve shirts
2 long-sleeve, long-body lightweight shirts
1 hooded sweatshirt
1 windbreaker/lightweight rain gear
1 pair slip-on plastic or cloth shoes for wet landings
2 pairs sturdy running shoes
1-week supply socks
1 large floppy hat with chin straps

TOILETRIES AND MEDICINE

Please note: If you are spending any time on mainland Ecuador, you must have a yellow fever/malaria vaccination, because Ecuador does have these diseases. Carry your proof of vaccination with you. Plan ahead on this, in case you have any adverse reaction to the vaccination. You don't want to have that while you are traveling.
1 large towel, 1 small towel, 1 face cloth

Toiletries (toothpaste, toothbrush, tampons, facial tissues, skin conditioner cream, etc.)

Sun block (as strong as possible), sunglasses (and strap to hold on in wind)

Shampoo (used for washing clothes as well as hair; saltwater soap not necessary)

12 large safety pins (diaper pins ideal)

Small first-aid kit (including bandages, antibiotic ointment, aspirin, sunburn or abrasion cream)

Medications you need. Take two sets of each if possible. Keep one set with you in your hand luggage on the plane. Pack the other. On the boat, keep the two sets in different places, and avoid carrying the whole supply with you at any one time.

Eyeglasses. Take two pairs and observe the same precautions as for medications.

Anti-seasickness medications: Consult your physician before using the seasickness patch. There have been reports of uncomfortable side effects from its use. I suggest just getting some over-the-counter dimenhydrinate pills and start taking them a couple of days before you sail; for the next 2 or 3 days take one every 4 hours during the day and at bedtime. Then test yourself without them on a short voyage. If you build it up in your system early on, you should be able to avoid discomfort. Most people find they don't need any help after the first 3 or 4 days. Certainly, that has been my experience, and I'm no natural-born sailer. If you forget these pills, any pharmacy in Quito will have the local equivalent. Just say, "Galapagos" and look queasy, and they will get the picture.

Protected against the glare of Caleta Tortuga Negra

Equipment

What equipment you bring reflects your own interests. In general, I suggest binoculars and camera(s), a small day pack for carrying film, towel, and other items when you're ashore, and an unbreakable water flask. Mask, snorkel, and fins are very useful, too, although they are provided on some boats now. Some people bring tape recorders and video equipment. Just remember that you will be getting on and off boats several times a day, so insure everything before you go and don't take anything you're not prepared to watch sink to the bottom of the ocean.

Scuba diving is a growing activity in the islands, but you must book with a boat that specializes in this and has the appropriate support systems, including the capacity to refill air tanks. The park service requires that the boat have a special naturalist guide who is also licensed as a diver. The boat must book an itinerary that concentrates on the diving sites, some of which are different from the sites for dry-landers. Some operators will arrange for dive opportunities using the local land based dive shops.

Passport

Make two photocopies of your passport and your tickets before you leave home. Leave one with your travel agent, and carry the other set of copies with you. If you lose your passport or tickets, it will be easier to overcome this problem if you have these photocopies as a record.

Money

Ecuador has moved to the U.S. dollar, so any conversion you do from your home currency will be on that basis. You simply use U.S. dollars everywhere, but prices in U.S. dollars are generally very low for items you buy. Many places do not accept $50 or $100 U.S. bills, by the way, so take smaller amounts with you or go to the nearest bank or cash machine—they are everywhere now.

You will want $5 to $10 U.S. per day to pay for cold drinks and beer on the boat. I suggest setting aside about 10 percent of the cost of your boat time for tips for the naturalist and crew. The tips usually are put into a kitty and given to the captain to distribute. Crew wages are usually low, and the tips are most welcome. You don't have to tip, but you probably will want to thank the crew and naturalist guide in this way. The chances are you will be extremely impressed and even touched by the expert and solicitous care you receive from the captain and crew.

As of early 2007, the Galapagos National Park fee is $100 per adult and $50 for children 11 years old and younger. This is payable upon your arrival at the airport in the Galapagos in U.S. dollars (cash only). Your tour operator certainly should be able to update you on any changes in this and make sure you are carrying the right kind and amount of cash for your various fees. In 2008 an extra $10 entry card is expected to be implemented. This is to help manage migration control—one of the most difficult challenges for protecting the islands

Don't forget there's also a $25 departure tax (cash only) from Ecuador. You pay this at the airport before you board your plane for home.

When you are in transit and in Quito, you can get cash on your credit card in banks in large cities and you can pay for services, meals, souvenirs, or other items by credit card and traveler's check in most establishments in Quito or Puerto Ayora on the islands. In smaller centers, credit cards and cash are preferred over traveler's checks. You will likely be charged an extra 10% on anything that you use a credit card for.

COMMUNICATIONS

When I first went to the islands, phone connections were risky at best and fax or other communications were very modest. Now international phoning on your card is easy. Or you can go to any of the myriad of "cabinas" where you can make international calls at just pennies a minute. There also is widespread access to the Internet. In Galapagos you can find email connections in little shops in Puerto Ayora on Santa Cruz and in Puerto Baquerizo Moreno on San Cristobal. We had a geologist on a recent trip, and he was able to access the Internet on his computer while on the boat. (I also used my computer on the boat, but just for word processing. The electricity is quite dependable, even if from a generator.)

In Quito there are many Internet cafes, and the ubiquitous phone cabinas, especially in the downtown international area. Each has its own special character and they're a lot of fun (also cheap, in North American terms, anyway). The assistants are very helpful, so don't worry if you speak little or no Spanish. The other patrons often speak English anyway, and they are generous with advice. These cafes also tend to be meeting places for international travelers and have bulletin boards about places to visit, shared rides, and rental accommodation. The cafe part varies from mostly beverages to full-fledged deli-style sandwiches and breakfasts.

Towns such as Otavalo have Internet cafes, and the cabinas too. One I went to in Otavalo was run by local Indian entrepreneurs. I was assisted by a very capable young woman in traditional dress as I sipped my hot chocolate and wrote to friends at home. I'm sure that by the time you read this all other towns of any size will have these cafes.

The Galapagos Islands are a utopia for wildlife photographers.

6
Notes on Photography

F irst, bring a camera and make sure you know how to use it. Digital cameras allow even the most inexperienced person to take pictures to be proud of. Just remember to bring plenty of batteries, though you can usually recharge in your hotel or on the boats. (Ecuador is on 110 volts, but the plug-ins are a bit hard to figure out. Bring a three-prong "cheater" along if you can.)

Having said that, if you prefer film-based cameras, but are not deeply involved with photography, the small, completely automatic cameras are excellent for taking scenery shots. If it has a zoom from 35 to 100mm or more, you'll be fine. You may not be able to do a close-up of a dozing iguana, but if there is a rock face littered with them, you can get a good picture. It will be a good camera for on-boat pictures of the group also.

If you are an experienced photographer, then you are in for one of the most exciting photographic adventures of your life. A 35-millimeter single lens reflex

Wildlife is so close in the islands that telephoto camera lenses aren't really necessary.

camera (or equivalent digital) will be your likely choice. For lenses, the essentials are a wide angle, a standard, and a moderate telephoto (300mm). If you like macro photography, then bring your favorite lens for that. The animal and birdlife is so close that a powerful telephoto lens is unnecessary and just means more weight (unless you use a lens that works for both telephoto and near-macro distances).

Above all, bring polarizing filters for every lens—or whatever you can do with your digital camera to cut glare through water. You will be taking pictures in highly reflective conditions and on and into water most of the time. You are seriously reducing your chances of good pictures by not having these filters.

If you are still using film, remember that even though you are at the equator, the Galapagos very often are under high cloud, and although you can get a bad sunburn, the available light for photography often is less than you would expect. So I suggest that you bring a range of film speeds, perhaps from 100 to 400 ASA.

As for the amount of film you will need, I take at least enough to use up three 36-exposure rolls per day. Just remember that you will be visiting two or more sites a day, you may want to take on-board shots at any time, and you will need addi-

Baby sea lions inspect a tourist's pack.

tional film if you travel on the mainland. So try to plan accordingly. Don't expect to buy film in Ecuador. It can be done, but you have no way of knowing how long it has been stored or under what conditions. So don't skimp; the Galapagos deserve your best. For digital, make sure your data chip in the camera holds at least 300 exposures, or you'll be constantly frustrated, and have your laptop or some other data storage system for downloading from your camera.

And if you're a film user, before you go, take all your film out of its boxes and mark the cartridge lids with indelible ink, noting the film speed and number of exposures per cartridge. Then put it in a strong clear plastic bag for taking it through airport inspections. Have the bag immediately accessible so you can easily hand it over to the attendant as you approach the x-ray machines. Sometimes you find attendants who don't want to cooperate, but be ready with the bag, smile, and stand firm.

Be sure to bring several of these sturdy plastic bags that you can close tightly. They are good for protecting your camera during sudden rains or for the trip between your boat and land. Once on your boat (or in the rainforest on the mainland), try to keep your film cool. On your land treks, take only the few rolls of film that you think you will use. Leave the rest in as low a location as possible in your cabin and wrap it in your clothes or a dry towel to provide some insulation against the heat. Check it periodically to see that it's not heating up.

If you are able to do little repairs on your camera, then bring the appropriate tools, especially a screwdriver that will allow general tightening of the equipment.

Be sure to start with new batteries for everything, and bring a replacement set. Also, lens-cleaning equipment is essential. There is a lot of humidity and sand to contend with.

APPENDIXES

A. QUITO AND MAINLAND ECUADOR

If you're planning to go as far as the Galapagos, I simply cannot emphasize how glad you will be if you take the time to visit some of mainland Ecuador. Ecuador is a magnificent country, extraordinarily varied in its geography, peoples, and natural and human history. It is beyond the scope of this book to give you detailed advice on mainland visiting, but there are books on travel in Ecuador that will be helpful. The ones aimed at backpackers often have the best information.

You will be arriving at and leaving from Quito, so at the very least spend time there. You should stay in one of the better "boutique" hotels used by local people and often locally owned. They are often family operations and are completely comfortable and well served. Unless you are ready to spend the same kind of money you spend in a downtown hotel in the United States or Europe for no better service, stay away from "international" hotels. They are good to visit to exchange your money, but otherwise a more modest approach to accommodation is best. Your travel agent should be able to help you here. The price range will be a good guide. (Aim for the middle.)

Also, if you book through a company that offers the boat tours, they will often be booking you into hotels in Quito. The price should be broken down by your agent, so you can see what you are paying for and can make comparisons.

Quito was built during Spanish colonial times. Its Old Quarter has been designated as a World Heritage Site by UNESCO. The Old Quarter is crowded and fascinating. There are regular tours you can take there, and it is an easy walk on your own once you take a taxi from the newer section of the city, where you probably will be staying.

You will feel quite safe in terms of courteous treatment from people, but picked pockets or snatched cameras or purses are becoming increasingly common in the old colonial part of the city. It's crowded there, with lots of people milling around on church steps and in narrow streets, so this kind of petty crime is fairly easy to carry out. (The market towns of Otavalo and Latacunga are beginning to acquire this reputation as well, unfortunately.) So take reasonable precautions, such as carrying most of your money in a sack around your neck under your shirt or in an extra pocket inside slacks. Don't carry free-hanging purses or cameras attached only by a little cord to your wrist. And avoid traveling alone at night. The newer sections of town seem to have fewer problems of this sort.

When you are in Quito, you are very likely to suffer a bit from the effects of suddenly arriving at high altitudes: headaches, tiring from the briefest walks, nausea, and difficulty sleeping. These symptoms will go away as soon as you get to sea level; acclimatization to Quito will occur within 2 or 3 days for most people. By walking slowly, eating moderately, drinking lots of fluids, and resting often, you should have little difficulty. The one other thing you might want to consider is taking a few sleeping pills for your Quito stay. Altitude sometimes makes people restive, and the city is noisy at night, particularly if you are in one of the small hotels or pensions in semi-residential areas. (I think every house has a barking German shepherd dog on guard.)

An absolute must for a 4- to 5-day trip out of Quito is an excursion to the Highlands, staying at various ones of the beautiful historic haciendas in the area; some are only a 2-hour drive from the capital. They provide a fascinating glimpse into the era of colonial settlement of the Andes.

I visited a number of different haciendas not far from Quito, drawing on the services of a local tour company, which provided a sparkling clean van, safe driver, and excellent multi-lingual guide. Each place we went was wonderful in its own way. In all cases the haciendas were beautifully renovated, completely comfortable inns. All meals were included. There were plenty of places to walk in the country-side, horseback riding was available, and the hosts were very helpful. The cost is about $100 U.S. per night per person, all included. (This is the most you should have to pay for any hotel in Ecuador.) Ask your travel agent, or one in Quito, about booking a stay in one of these beautiful places. There are also eco-lodges in the Highlands. I stayed in Tambopaxi Lodge, on the plains of Mt. Cotopaxi, and was just entranced by the whole experience.

On our Highlands jaunt, led by our very skilled guide, we also stopped in various villages and saw up close some of the local industries (weaving, musical instruments, dough-doll making, etc.), chatted with the residents and workers and had a very pleasant and illuminating time. Naturally, you will have a chance to buy locally-made weavings or instruments or other gifts for yourself and your friends back home. It's all very comfortable and low-key—you won't be pressured to do so. It's almost like dropping in on new acquaintances and learning a bit about their lives (and probably vice versa).

If you have only 1 or 2 free days in Quito and you are a birdwatcher, you can arrange for an all-day excursion to a cloud forest nature refuge. These are on the western slope of the Andes, at about 1000 meters elevation. There are several only a few hours' drive from Quito or Guayaquil. These lodges and their grounds are a paradise for birdwatchers. Again, your tour operator or a local tourism office in Quito can direct you to one of these places. You will see ads for them in the Internet cafes and other places frequented by tourists.

On one of my last trips, because of delays caused by volcanic activity, my land tour operator arranged this brief excursion for me. I spent a day at Bella Vista Lodge, a wonderful rustic lodge, and was driven there by the lodge's own taxi service. The 2-

hour ride in was a dazzling exposure to the countryside around Quito: precipitous gorges, waterfalls, and changes from wet to dry microhabitats. At the lodge we had breakfast and then the owner took us out for a 4-hour bird walk along rugged paths. The birding was fantastic, and the late lunch was excellent. Then the ride back to Quito was mostly for resting. It is possible to take trips into the Amazon area, a rich sweep of rainforest that clothes the eastern side of the Ecuadorian Andes. I've been to lodges there several times and have found the accommodations to be comfortable, the food good, the guides excellent, and the environment superb. Your travel agent will be able to help you make arrangements, or a nature club or nature tour organization may run tours from your home city. I suggest pre-booking if possible, but you can book a trip once you are in Quito. Ask at your hotel how to contact the agent. If you leave yourself several days in Quito before your departure for the Galapagos, you should be able to reserve a trip for when you return. The usual duration of one of these trips is 4 or 5 days.

Some Summary Comments on Travel in Ecuador

If overall impressions can be depended upon, I can unequivocally state that in my six visits and 12 weeks in the Ecuadorian mainland over 24 years, there was only one time when I was not made to feel completely welcome, safe, comfortable, and fairly and openly treated in all financial exchanges. This was due to an over-zealous young militiaman, who somehow thought my well-dressed teenage nephews should show him identification while we were strolling in a park. Our guide was a few steps away, saw what was happening, and brought this little event to an abrupt halt. (There is a lot to be said for having a guide, even for day trips in the city. You will learn more, enjoy the guide's company, and avoid misunderstandings of any sort. I highly recommend this for those who prefer the "no surprises" approach to travel, especially those with limited time.) I tend to travel on a modest scale, using good, locally patronized hotels and pensiones. They may have been fairly expensive by local standards but were quite reasonable for a North American. I was with a large group on one trip, although we often went off on our own in groups of two or three. Otherwise, in Quito, I was on my own or with one or two friends. I took taxis and walked around town on my own during the day and in the early evening—in busy parts of downtown, but not in the Old City or in residential areas. On two visits I also booked through the Quito-based land tour operator a minivan and driver for 3 days and nights in the Highlands, staying in various haciendas (which cost about $80 U.S. a day for transportation, guide and driver, and meals along the way several years ago. It will be more now, but still should be within what I see as a very reasonable range). Both trips were marvelous. It was an efficient use of my time and it was wonderful to have a bilingual guide who was familiar with local culture and was very helpful with the frequent side trips and stops we made for birding.

As for languages: if your Spanish can meet the challenge of counting to 10 and then by hundreds, if you can use standard pleasantries for time of day, for the bill ("la cuenta, por favor"), and for "thank you" and "please," and if you are prepared to smile when things go a little more slowly than you expect, you will be fine. The firm, almost authoritarian approach that gets things done in North America or Europe is ineffective in Ecuador. People just melt away. So smile and throw yourself on people's mercy, and their deeply ingrained politeness and kindness will have an opportunity to express itself fully.

B. Suggested Reading

There is so much to read on the Galapagos that I'm going to suggest just a few basics. One is Darwin's *Voyage of the Beagle,* of course, and there are two excellent bird guides. The standby since the mid-1970s has been *The Collins Field Guide to the Birds of Galapagos* by Michael Harris (Stephen Greene Press, 1989). A newer one is *A Guide to Birds of the Galapagos Islands* by Isabel Castro, with Antonia Phillips (Princeton University Press, 1996). Daniel Fitter's *Wildlife of the Galapagos* is highly recommended (Safari Guides).

Your main sources for reading materials will be the Internet, your bookstore, or your library. In your Internet search, check out the many newsletters, research reports, and annual plans and reports from the Charles Darwin Foundation (*www.darwinfountation.org*), the park service, and other partners such as the World Wildlife Fund. You will probably have done an extensive amount of background reading before you go, and most of it will enhance your trip. But there are some bookstores in Quito, and some in Guayaquil, where you can get some interesting local or international bird guidebooks, plant guides, and historical and cultural overviews of Ecuador and its people. The best-known and largest store is Libri Mundi, but keep your eyes open for the smaller ones, which often have their own distinctive inventory.

C. Information for Galapagos Supporters

The Charles Darwin Foundation is dependent on donations to carry out its work. It is largely dependant on individual donors for the funds needed to finance its research, education, and restoration programs, especially as the support it used to receive from various international organizations has diminished in today's world of changing priorities—with conservation being less high on the priority list of former international sources of support. The Galapagos National Park Service itself is supported by visitors in great part by the entry fees paid upon arrival. There is an active Friends of Galapagos network of organizations that support the Charles Darwin Foundation. To become a Friend of the Galapagos, send contributions in U.S. funds to the following address (check or money order; tax receipt provided for contributions over $25):

Galapagos Conservancy (formerly The Charles Darwin Foundation, Inc.)
407 North Washington St., Suite 105
Falls Church, Virginia 22046
email: darwin@galapagos.org
Membership manager: comments@galapagos.org
Telephone: 1-703-538-6833
website: *www.galapagos.org*

I hope you will find your own way of supporting the islands, which are a gift to us all. Our contributions play a major role in making sure that gift will be there in the future.

Welcome sign

TRIP LOG

	BIRDS	MAMMALS	FISH
DAY 1			
DAY 2			
DAY 3			
DAY 4			
DAY 5			
DAY 6			
DAY 7			

PLANTS	REPTILES	NOTES

INDEX

About the Author

Marylee Stephenson has been a dedicated amateur naturalist for most of her adult life, starting as a birdwatcher and expanding her interests over time. Along with the guidebook to the Galapagos, she has written a visitor's guide to the national parks of Canada, which went through three editions and was published in three languages. From time to time she publishes in magazines and appears on radio.

Marylee has a doctorate in sociology and operates her own consulting company (*www.csresors.com*), which specializes in program evaluation and research and policy analysis on a wide range of topics. Marylee has taken up standup comedy over the last several years and is active in clubs and as a conference and workshop presenter across Canada (*www. sociocomic.com*). This still leaves her time for travel, and she is finalizing her seventh trip to the Galapagos and mainland Ecuador as this revised edition of the guidebook goes to press.

THE MOUNTAINEERS, founded in 1906, is a nonprofit outdoor activity and conservation club, whose mission is "to explore, study, preserve, and enjoy the natural beauty of the outdoors . . . . " Based in Seattle, Washington, the club is now one of the largest such organizations in the United States, with seven branches throughout Washington State.

The Mountaineers sponsors both classes and year-round outdoor activities in the Pacific Northwest, which include hiking, mountain climbing, ski-touring, snowshoeing, bicycling, camping, kayaking and canoeing, nature study, sailing, and adventure travel. The club's conservation division supports environmental causes through educational activities, sponsoring legislation, and presenting informational programs. All club activities are led by skilled, experienced volunteers, who are dedicated to promoting safe and responsible enjoyment and preservation of the outdoors.

If you would like to participate in these organized outdoor activities or the club's programs, consider a membership in The Mountaineers. For information and an application, write or call The Mountaineers, Club Headquarters, 7700 Sand Point Way NE, Seattle, WA 98115; 206-521-6001.

The Mountaineers Books, an active, nonprofit publishing program of the club, produces guidebooks, instructional texts, historical works, natural history guides, and works on environmental conservation. All books produced by The Mountaineers Books fulfill the club's mission.

Send or call for our catalog of more than 500 outdoor titles:

The Mountaineers Books
1001 SW Klickitat Way, Suite 201
Seattle, WA 98134
800-553-4453
mbooks@mountaineersbooks.org
www.mountaineersbooks.org